SQUEEZED
Rear-Ended by American Politics

J.C. Bourque

Snarkiman Publishing
Denver

ACKNOWLEDGEMENTS

A number of people contributed things large and small to this book. Some of them don't even realize it. I hesitate to acknowledge someone's contribution to a book about politics unless they've agreed to it beforehand, in case the book is wildly denounced as heretic nonsense or offensive dribble, and they would prefer not to be associated with it. On the other hand, anyone who knows that you are writing what you hope will be a controversial (and therefore widely-selling) book about the subject of American politics should know better than to talk to you at all, lest they end up as embarrassing examples. Nevertheless, it seems only fair to spare them the indignity.

Others are members of my family, specifically, mom and dad— Marilyn and Jim, my sister Barbara, and my brother Tom. They are unfortunate enough to be related to me, and certainly should be immune to the accompanying public humiliation by now, so they have no choice but to be included here. They each read and commented helpfully on an early draft. They also refrained from rolling their eyes and sighing resignedly in my company.

Two people offered to edit a subsequent draft, and their generous assistance reduced the odds of both heretic nonsense and offensive dribble (or drivel, for that matter) being included. Probably some other embarrassing stuff as well. These are Rexford Brown and Gary Keene. Both were warned that they would appear here.

Once the big cow-pies were removed with the help of those two, Cathy Bodine, PhD. performed an extremely-detailed, multi-pass edit that helped me polish this into the sparkling jewel that you now hold. Heartfelt thanks for your help, Cathy.

I never tried to write a book before. This is a lot of work. Many people who take on something like this get a grant or have a patron to keep them from staving during the process. I wasn't so lucky.

I was luckier. Lisa Heppner is my life and business partner, best friend and sweetheart. She kept our businesses going, helped me through moments of doubt, laughed at the funny parts, and contributed many ideas, refinements and punch lines that are included here. And made sure I didn't starve. It would not have been possible to do this without her support. Lisa, I appreciate it more than I can say, or have said, and I love you.

INTRODUCTION.

I don't believe that Heaven and Hell actually exist, and at present I'm not willing to die to find out. However, one can never be sure about such things. If it turns out that I'm wrong, I *am* certain of this: I will be going to Hell.

I speculate that *if* Hell is real it will be custom-made for each Sinner, to maximize Eternal Suffering. The Fiery Furnace, for example, sounds pretty horrible to me, but might not seem terribly punitive to a serial arsonist. In his case, it might be more effective to set him loose in a boundless City of Kindling— with no matches or accelerants to be found anywhere. And a fire station on every block. Frustrate the asshole for eternity.

I imagine my Personal Hell would be something like this: there are two rooms, each infinite in size. Inside each room are an infinite number of people, and all of them are lecturing, hectoring, chastising, squabbling with and proselytizing— to me. They are doing this because each one of them believes that he alone possesses the Answers to Everything Important in Life, and feels compelled to persuade me to adopt his beliefs— whether I like it or not.

Each room has one door in, and one door out. When I can no longer stand being tortured in one room, I can enter the other room, but with the horrifying knowledge that the haranguing will be equally unendurable. The only difference will be the subject material. When the pain becomes unbearable in the second room, I have but one choice: to reenter the first.

In one room is a perpetual MoveOn.org rally; the other, a perpetual Tea Party protest. For Eternity, I will be tortured by a countless number of passionate extremists and true believers getting in my face.

Perhaps I'm in Hell already.

SQUEEZED BY WHAT?

Two groups of people are starting to really irritate the hell out of me. Actually, that's not accurate. They've been pissing me off for quite some time. They are:

    A. Right-Wing Extremists
    B. Left-Wing Extremists

At first glance, these two groups might seem so different that they shouldn't be the subject of the same book, but as I will show, they are more alike than either of them would like to contemplate. Although these groups push (and push) very different agendas, from the point of view of the Guy In The Middle (me), it's their similarities that are most irritating. The most important of these similarities is that they are both pushing agendas. At me. And I'm tired of it.

Here are the folks I'm talking about, as defined by their *differences:*

The first category, Right-Wing Extremists (RWEs, hereafter) are people who are afraid of change, frightened by human nature, terrified of Socialism or hinky about sex and feel a compelling need to share these feelings with the rest of us. These may be AM-radio shriek jocks continually blathering about Barack Obama's birth certificate, the ever-impending Marxist Threat, or a host of other perceived attacks upon the American Way.

Alternatively, they might be televangelist, Bible-thumping, morality-police types who have received the Word of God (somehow) and are compelled by faith to spread their idea of morality to everyone.[1]

Because every one of these religious nutballs interprets his Divine Guidance differently, we Unwashed are subject to an unending barrage of conflicting versions of God's Will by which we are supposed to abide. One feature they all seem to share is a deeply ingrained fear of human nature, and they are determined to force a standard of conforming behavior on the rest of us, in the vain hope that this might

---

1 I have intentionally left out Neo-Nazi, white-supremacist wack jobs who can't get jiggy with the fact that we're all Ethiopians if you go back far enough. Those people are so far out there that they need to be the subject of another book. By someone else.

help them control *themselves*. To accomplish this, it is necessary to ruthlessly suppress most of the features that make people interesting, and in particular, anything to do with sex.

At the other end of the spectrum are the Left-Wing Extremists (LWEs). These are people who consider themselves intellectually superior to the rest of us and, because of this, believe it is their job to engineer a perfect society for us all to inhabit. Whether they possess the proper credentials and wisdom to overhaul society is irrelevant; in the LWE world view, intellectual prowess in *any* subject conveys equal prowess in *all* subjects.

LWEs consider it their mission to promote, celebrate and revel in the same aspects of human nature that the RWEs are trying to suppress. Any form of shocking, depraved or perverted behavior is acceptable, even encouraged, particularly if it serves the added purpose of making RWEs appear to be squeamish, provincial or prudish.

LWEs also revere the concept of "Diversity," which is the celebration of the idea of a glorious rainbow of human variation— except for white people. Ironically, most of those doing the celebrating are white people who live in secluded, white-people enclaves such as college campuses.

Perversely, it is also part of the LWEs' strategy to simultaneously pretend to be unaware of a significant number of differences in human nature that cannot (so far, anyway) be bred out of us, such as skin color, gender, height, weight, intelligence, beauty and age; and behaviors such as greed, hatred, warmongering, disparate earning potential, cultural bias for or against hard work and— perhaps their most-hated— people's desire to congregate into groups and prevent those "other people" from moving in next door. Lots of these "open minded" people live in places like Portland— recently named "Whitest city in America." However, as I mentioned earlier, anything to do with sex is totally cool.

Members of these two extremist groups may "mean well," but so what? None of them feels the need to consult the rest of us before implementing their Grand Vision. Our own thoughts, feelings, desires, knowledge, experience, preferences or (God forbid) *vision* of what is best for us is irrelevant.

You can't necessarily recognize these people on the street— they look pretty much like the rest of us. It's their beliefs and behaviors that define them. When (if) you finish reading this book, you'll be able to recognize them everywhere. Unfortunately. Then you'll be as pissed off as I am.

We can learn a lot about these two groups by analyzing the responses that the following statement engenders in each:

"The President got a blow job from an intern."

The RWEs have a problem with this for several reasons:

- The idea of anyone getting a blow job bothers them from a morality (read: jealousy) standpoint;
- The term "blow job" makes them uncomfortable;[2]
- The President is not married to the intern, hence his behavior is "sinful";
- A Presidential blow job is not a good example to set for our children;
- They think this behavior is rather unseemly for the Leader of the Free World.

The LWEs don't know whether they have a problem with this or not, until they have the answers to several important questions:

- Is the President a Republican or a Democrat?
- Does the blow job adversely affect the President's ability to lead the Free World?[3]
- Is the intern "hot"?

---

2 Blow job.   Blow job.   Blowjobblowjobblowjobblowjobblowjob.

3 This has become known as "The Maher Interrogatory."

- Does the President support a Woman's Right to Choose?[4]

- Has the French or Italian President already gotten a blow job from an intern?

In short, RWEs have a rigid concept of morality and a flaccid idea of sex, while the LWEs are the polar opposite.

Many other traits, behaviors, and beliefs distinguish these groups from one other, and some of them will be addressed as we proceed. However, since it's their similarities that are the primary subject here, we'll focus on exploring some of the more-formidable ones that make life less bountiful and more unpleasant for the typical Middle.

First, a definition is in order. A Middle, in the context of this book, is a person who is not a member of either of these two political groups, but isn't really a member of any particular other group either. We're political leftovers— people who are held in contempt by both RWEs and LWEs because of our failure to "see the light," "get it," or otherwise give a shit about their pet issues. I don't use the traditional labels for people like us such as "Moderate," "MOR" or "Centrist." These terms fail to convey the sense of helpless predicament— the "civilian-caught-in-the-crossfire" aspect— that accompanies life in the middle of the street battle being waged by these two groups. Therefore, I hope to establish the term "Guy In The Middle" or, "Middle" for short, as the name for the sociopolitical group that I claim to represent. (For the record: Who elected me? I did.)

Second, a disclaimer: this rant is not about people who quietly practice their faith or follow their beliefs without pushing their views on others. A few of those folks were offended while reading early drafts of this book, so I want to make it clear that if you're not in my face about your viewpoint, you're not the subject here.

Now that the housekeeping is done, let's get started on the fun stuff.

---

4 The real question should be: Does the President support a woman's right to choose NOT to be cowed into servicing the most-powerful man on Planet Earth, in the most power-imbalanced work relationship *ever* devised, if she doesn't want to?

THE COMFORTING WORLD VIEWS
OF THE EXTREMISTS

Extremists prefer nice, uncomplicated binary world views. This way of thinking is attractive because it provides valuable cognitive benefits:

- **You don't need to think very much or very often.** Really, what is more irritating than to get up in the morning and feel compelled to make fresh, new observations about the world around you? — Again. By utilizing a binary world view, you don't need to be bothered with all that.

- **You can easily identify the Good Guys and Bad Guys.** What a pain in the ass to have to learn enough about each individual to make a special, personalized character judgment. Who's got the time? Are you Pro-life or a baby murderer? Are you against the war or an imperialist pig? That's all you need to know about someone. See how simple it can be?

- **Binary world views provide comfort.** False and fleeting comfort, unfortunately for the rest of us. That's why extremists are always in our face. Deep down, they know their philosophy is flawed, unsupportable, unverifiable or fragile. One way to feel better about betting the farm on a weak hand is to get people like me to agree that it was a good idea. If they can persuade us to adopt their belief system by proselytizing, it takes away some of their uncertainty. Temporarily.

Middles don't need to attend rallies or weekly services. Each day provides a rich and tasty stew of information that supports our world view.[5] Extremists, on the other hand, need continual reinforcement of their belief systems to keep them magically suspended high above the hard, rocky ground of reality.

---

5 Which will be discussed in detail later but is, essentially, that life is a rich and tasty stew of ambiguity, randomness, and difficulty that you must slog through whether you like it or not.

The binary world view helps keep at bay a host of uncomfortable feelings, ideas and thoughts that threaten the belief system: things like doubt, temptation, contradictory evidence and the fact that nonbelievers seem to be having a whole lot more fun (and are getting blow jobs.) The binary world view is the glue that holds the disparate pieces of the philosophy in place, and fills the gaps and holes between the pieces from which faith and commitment are constantly leaking.

Here's a snapshot of the two primary binary world views that dominate our political system:

PARTY OF THE VICTIM VS.
PARTY OF THE PERPETRATOR.

This, the staple of the LWE, divides society into two groups:

The Victims: Honest, "hardworking" people of all colors but one, and all sexual orientations but one, who love the Earth, endorse Fairness and Equality, have at least one close friend of an obviously different race and/or culture,[6] and who, despite their selfless work on behalf of world peace, social justice, and redistribution of everything, are continually being screwed over by conspiratorial institutions run by

The Perpetrators: Greedy White Males (hereafter, GreedyWhiteMales or GWMs). These people are responsible for everything bad that has ever happened to anyone.

Party mission: These GreedyWhiteMales must be stopped, before it's TOO LATE.

PARTY OF THE ENLIGHTENED VS.
PARTY OF THE MORALLY DEPRAVED.

This, the RWE world view, also divides society into two groups:

The Enlightened: Persons of high moral character who are the recipients of a body of Divine Guidance regarding every aspect of life,

---

6 As an alternative to having actual ethnic friends, one can go to a Third World Country as part of a government program or foreign-study exchange, eat weird food while sitting on a dirt floor, and return a "Permanently Changed Person Whose Eyes Have Been Opened To The Injustices Perpetrated On The World By Our Corrupt, Colonialist Government."

coupled with— (sorry, poor choice of words)— *married to* a Charter from Heaven to stop all these *other* people,

The Morally Depraved: from doing all those disgusting, reprehensible, vile, endlessly-fascinating things that they so obviously enjoy, and who— because they are enjoying them so much— irritate the shit out of the Enlightened Persons. "Those perverts are having just too darned much fun, and besides, it's really hard *not* to want to watch Hot Lesbian Action on SkineMax."

Party Mission: These Morally Depraved people must be stopped, before it's TOO LATE.

MY FELLOW AMERICANS: PLEASE PUT A SOCK IN IT.

Activists can't shut up. They are compelled to stop you at the supermarket and persuade you to sign a petition regarding some obscure issue that they are all spun up about. And no matter the subject, it is always an "emergency" or "outrage." To raise your awareness, they will put you on e-mail "action alerts," directing you to various ranting blog sites. They leaflet your car ("Save the Trees!"), and knock on your door to tell you about their religion. They block city streets with protest marches when I'm desperately trying to get to Starbucks (screw the war— I need caffeine!). They will never leave people like me alone, because all "True Believers" need to convert others to their cause, and no matter how hard they try to accomplish this, people like me "just don't get it." This drives them shithouse.

These are people who think it makes sense to bomb a Hummer dealership in the name of environmentalism. Or they think Satan has infested their children through pop music.[7] Some refuse to have their children vaccinated because— well, I have no idea why they would do such a thing. But they have managed to resurrect whooping cough in several places— a disease that was essentially eradicated from this country when my grandmother was a child. Huzzah!

---

7 This is mistaken: Satan has infested their children through their Pee-Pees, as he has for eons. They cannot accept this.

On the other hand, I, as a Middle, am perfectly capable of leaving all activists completely alone without compromising my lifestyle one whit. Really. When I get up in the morning it never occurs to me to get dressed, go outside, and accost strangers on the street to wag my finger in their faces.

Mow them down, yes.

HOW DID I GET SO IRRITATED?

Perhaps at this point you're wondering:

"Wow, how did he get so snarky about this stuff?" or,

"Wow, how can I get a refund of the perfectly good money I spent on this book?"

As to the second question: you probably can't. That's one of the few great things about the publishing industry. You can't usually return a book just because it sucks from a literary standpoint. The cover has to come unglued, or something like that.

As to the first question, I first got my knickers in a twist about this stuff during the 2004 Presidential Election. That election was so polarized and nasty[8] that I started to feel ashamed to be an American, although not for any of the reasons suggested by the Presidential candidates. Not only were the candidates and the media getting into the fray, ordinary citizens were hurling invective at one other and fighting as if their lives were at stake. I was genuinely concerned that I would lose friends over disagreements about the election.

Another negative feature was the crude fucking level of discourse that many people were employing in the process. Rather than debating the merits of the candidates' positions, people simply dismissed those with a differing point of view as beneath contempt. Red-state Idiot. Whiny Liberal. Warmonger. Chickenshit.

---

8 Little did I know what was coming ...

However, there was one political viewpoint even more despicable than either conservative or liberal— one kind of voter more reviled, dangerous and more clearly clueless than any partisan:

Undecided.

In the run-up to the 2004 election (commencing, as you may recall, in 2002), there was no better way to piss off someone than to describe yourself as an Undecided Voter. Judging by people's responses, this was tantamount to trafficking in kiddie porn. Maybe worse. Whenever I described myself as an undecided voter, I was lambasted by conservatives and liberals alike. The essence of their argument was that the issues were so clear, and the choice between candidates so obvious, that the only plausible explanation for my "undecidedness" was that I was either stupid or was maliciously trying to irritate everyone.

Comedian and TV producer Larry David wrote a New York Times guest editorial about people like me, explaining the reasons we "pretended" to be undecided:

- It makes us feel powerful when we can ruin the mood at dinner parties.
- We like the attention we get by goading others into apoplectic rage.
- We enjoy watching them (the "Decideds") talk themselves silly trying to convince us to vote for their candidate.

It was inconceivable to Mr. David that someone would prefer to wait until November 2nd to decide.

As an Unelected Representative of Undecided Voters Everywhere, I can assure you that we don't enjoy being lectured by angry partisans. Believe me, no rational person would willingly subject himself to the certainty of verbal abuse by simply engaging in conversation. But that's what Mr. David thought people like me were doing. This would be like finding a magic lantern and choosing— as your single wish— to be the subject of a Senate investigation.

"It's a simple question, Mr. Bourque, and this Panel deserves a straight answer: Are you an asshole or an idiot?"

And choosing this because it "sounded like fun."

Further, no, we don't like ruining dinner parties, either. It's just that we "Undecideds" weren't willing to acquiesce to the New Purpose of dinner parties: political bullying and thought remediation. We thought it was for a bunch of friends to get together and have a few laughs.

"Senator, as I've tried to explain, and believe the facts support, I'm both."

I can also tell you that the "attention" is no fun, either. I got plenty of this kind of attention in school. At the time they called it "going to the Principal's office."

Mr. David summed up his piece by explaining how irritating it was to talk to people like me— who either failed to grasp the crystalline obviousness of his reasoning, or were purposely ruining his evening by remaining undecided.

I think people like *him* are irritating. For one thing, they're the ones who won't stop talking about politics. Don't want your dinner party ruined? Stop bringing up the election— especially if you think everyone should have decided by now. But they bring it up anyway for two reasons:

- So they can use their Intellectual Prowess and Powerful Grasp of the Issues to slice up dissenting party guests; and/or

- To reinforce solidarity with those who agree with them.

One thing no partisan ever expected was to trip over an Actual Undecided Voter. Of course, one (me, anyway) might think that all their beautifully crafted policy arguments were specifically intended for this kind of situation, and that an open-minded and lively conversation about the issues would ensue, but one (again— me, anyway) would be mistaken. These days, political rhetoric is used only for beating up people. Every four years, Americans are presented with an opportunity to show how much more aware, moral, astute, concerned, informed and enlightened they are than, for example—

You.

Here's my gripe with Mr. Comedian-*cum*-Commentator: If he enjoys the certainty that *anyone* in his party is a better candidate for office than *everyone* in the opposition party, that's fine. However, categorizing me as clueless or malevolent just because I'd prefer to wait until Election Day to pull the lever reveals a nasty closed-mindedness on his part. I'm sorry he finds it irritating, but I can't state with complete confidence that I know who should be the President of the United States in a year (or two), and I see no reason I should be compelled to commit today.

Given that the role of the President is largely managerial (theoretically, anyway. It *is* called the Executive Branch), why should I be compelled today to choose the person who should be managing affairs in another year? I have no idea what affairs will need to be managed by then, and neither does anyone else— comedians, perhaps, in particular. Even if I have a preference today, it could change with tomorrow's headlines. One candidate might be a good day-to-day manager and another preferable during an emergency. It's my right to wait to choose the best person for the task at hand, and no one's business to give me a hard time about my choices or my timetable for making them.

I believe that contemporaneous circumstances have a huge impact on the decision regarding who should helm the ship. And I can think of a *very* long list of politicians that I *do not* want in the White House when that killer comet is headed our way.

Besides, dirty pictures of your beloved candidate might surface tomorrow morning, deep-sixing his campaign by mid afternoon. And there *are* dirty pictures of your candidate. Bank on it.

REDUXIO AD ABSURDUM

Now it's summer 2011, and Here We Go Again. Congress and the President are in meetings at the White House pretending that they *really might* let the country default. Republican and Democrat leaders are digging in on key "non-negotiables" in order to preen for the electorate. President Obama goes on TV and hints that Social Security checks "might not go out." Bullshit. They aren't going to let us go broke. They're all milking the situation for maximum press coverage.

Next we get James "Skeletor" Carville flapping on about the crisis, saying exactly what we already know he's going to say: It's all the Republicans' fault, and the Democrats are a bunch of fucking saints who are "just trying to save the country."

Meanwhile, Michelle Bachmann is backpedaling about her husband being in the "Cure gays through prayer" business, and the press is begrudgingly giving her credit for "forming complete sentences." Sarah Palin is sitting on a high branch like Snoopy pretending to be a vulture, waiting to swoop down and announce her candidacy, threatening us with the specter of a primary debate between two conservative airheads. What are they going to debate? Whether a Mama Grizzly is scarier than a Mama Tiger?[9]

And of course our President has shattered yet another fund raising record, which now— thanks to the Patriot Stephen Colbert— can be augmented by the Media spending its own airtime shilling for candidates without reporting it as a campaign contribution. The Presidency is now, officially, Up For Sale. For a cool Billion.

Political discourse— a thought-provoking exchange of viewpoints intended to enlighten the perspectives of all participants— can be enjoyable and rewarding, but that's not how it works in today's polarized and hostile climate. It has instead become an opportunity for angry, bitter partisans to ceaselessly lecture their friends, coworkers, fellow bar patrons and family members about how stupid they are if they don't agree with the lecturer.

---

9 She has since decided to sit this one out. Whew...

Partisans offer only two intellectual positions in the current climate of debate:

- Agree with me enthusiastically by parroting everything I say, or,
- Shut up while I explain how stupid you are for disagreeing with my cogent and brilliant analysis of the situation.

If you choose option number two, you attain a special status in American political discourse:

You're an idiot.

Of course, all of this hostile rhetoric is predicated on the flagrant falsehood that we Americans *want* to be well informed about politics (or anything else, for that matter) and that this desire for enlightenment explains why we like to talk about it so much. My observation is that most people aren't, and don't really want to be, well informed about the subject. They just like to argue, so they can *win* at something. That's why they repeat obvious bullshit "information" about political candidates, ignore factual but negative press about their favorite ones, and forward countless morsels of unsubstantiated Internet drivel to one another. For most, the election is just another game, like the Super Bowl®:

- Two teams;
- Don't get caught on penalty plays;
- Winner takes all;
- The other guys are jerks.

(One significant difference is what happens when players change teams. In football, they get new uniforms. In politics, switching teams is unforgivable. Just ask Joe Lieberman.)

WHAT GETS INTO THESE PEOPLE?

If you're a Middle, you might be asking yourself:

"Why do these people think the way they do?" or,

"How can people believe that crap?" or,

"Who's ringing the doorbell this time?"

Don't answer it. It's someone with more pamphlets.

Meanwhile, let's have a detailed look at some of the attributes that make it possible for a person to be an activist/extremist/reformer. This discussion will be divided into six sections:

- BEHAVIOR TRAITS
- BELIEF SYSTEMS
- COGNITIVE TRAPS
- OPERATIONAL METHODOLOGIES
- TOOLS AND TACTICS
- SCHMOLITICS

One thing you may notice about the next section of the book is that I do not make much of a distinction between the RWE and the LWE. This is because from the point-of-view of the Middle, *the extreme left and right are functionally equivalent,* in that they both believe they know what is best for us, and will never stop trying to tell us how to live our lives. Let's explore some of the irritating, self-righteous traits that these two groups of people have in common.

Part One:

BEHAVIOR TRAITS

The notion that these two groups have more similarities than differences had been simmering in my head for a while, but a catalyst was required for this notion to fuse into a philosophy (of sorts). That catalyst was provided when the Democratic Party nominated a candidate— John Kerry— who sucked as much as the incumbent, George W. Bush, who sucked about as much as can be imagined. It was a deeply mystifying moment.

Liberal partisans had, by this time, firmly established that they believed Dubya was, if not The Worst President Of All Time,[1] at least a major contender for the honor.[2] One would think that the moment had arrived to strike a death blow to the Republican Party, but one (as we will see many times in the following pages) would be wrong.

The Dems, despite being handed the opportunity of the eon, did what they always do— look in Massachusetts for some rich guy. Ted was off drinking somewhere, so they said to themselves: "Maybe there's someone with lackluster speaking skills, negative charisma, no firm positions, and who looks like shit in wet-suit." They found one— placing me in the position of having no one to vote for in either party.

I was an undecided voter.

What I did not anticipate was that I had unwittingly become the sworn enemy of both types of partisans. In the ensuing months, politically inflamed people of both parties began to behave as if my single, piddling vote held the key to the survival of civilization. I began to experience bipartisan bantering, battering, berating and bludgeoning on an epic scale.

None of these amateur partisan lobbyists showed the slightest interest in my views regarding the candidates, platforms or policies in the race. It was all, and only, about converting my vote. Eventually it became obvious to me that both groups behaved essentially the same. I was a man alone.

---

1 I'm still going with Grover Cleveland.

2 The official confirmation of this title would not come until his second term.

However, being a man without a Party results in a lot of free time, and I used it to start cataloging the behaviors that these two groups of extremists have in common. Herewith, a sampling.

I'M A HAMMER, LOOKING FOR A NAIL. CONGRATULATIONS— YOU'RE THE NAIL!

A Painter paints. A Farmer farms. A Reformer… well, reforms.

Around the globe, there are certain people who reach a point in their lives when they decide that they have a "better idea" for how to do things. Many of these, after experiencing this "enlightenment," limit their resultant activity to animated discussions with friends over coffee, wine, spliffs or hookas, while perusing partisan tracts late into the night, when they vow to change their lives in profound and meaningful ways first thing in the morning. Then they get up and go back to work like everyone else. No harm is done.

However, a subset of these people ratchets it up a notch or two and become "Reformers," "Activists," "True Believers," "Extremists" and other virulent life forms. They might act upon this newfound enlightenment by starting a new religion, campaigning for (or against) something, founding an NGO or going to Washington to become a Public Servant. Once they get up and running, you can jolly well expect some reforming activity to take place.

The reform process can often be complex and multifaceted, utilizing many skills and disciplines such as fund-raising, pamphleteering, demonstrating, haranguing, press conferencing and other stuff. I could provide an overview of the reforming art, the skill sets needed, and the dedicated people who devote their energies to Great Causes, blah, blah— but I'll spare you all that, because you only need to know a couple of things about it to determine how tightly you should pucker up:

- Reforming, by its nature, requires a *Status Quo*.
- That *Status Quo*, my friend, is YOU. And your lifestyle. And everything you stand for.

Just as the architect "lives" to design a new building, the Reformer exists to design a New Paradigm. So, if you happen to be happy with your selfish, shallow, meaningless and pathetic little existence, bend over— Reform is headed your way.

During this "reform" process, you are going to be prodded, cajoled, interrogated, harassed, criticized, defamed, denounced, inquisitioned, strip-searched and anal-probed (metaphorically), challenged, accused, blamed, and/or tried and convicted (again, metaphorically, if not actually) while being deluged with misquoted factoids, twisted statistics, irrational ranting, fear-mongering theoretical scenarios, baseless paranoid claims, urban mythology and outright lies— all issuing forth from countless newsletters, web sites, blogs, protesters, proselytizers, pundits, expert witnesses, newscasters, politicians and ill-informed partisan wackos. (If you need to take a smoke break at this point, I understand. I'll be right here when you get back.)

And it doesn't stop there. Before the current cohort of Reformers has finished with you, a Brand New Generation of Reformers will spring forth, yanking out the freshly minted World-Changing, Exciting New Paradigm (soon to be known as the "You-Can't-Have-Been-Serious-Paradigm") that has been only partially thrust up your life, and replacing it with an even-newer New Paradigm— known as the Post-New, Double-Enlightened Universe-Altering Paradigm (soy milk; no whip, please). No paradigm will be fully implemented before being itself yanked out, to be replaced by yet another new start-up paradigm (typically by the opposition, who are now in power again due to the predictable mid-term election bloodbath) producing the single outcome of each party compiling a long list of failures to attribute to meddling interference by the other side.

At this point you may be suffering from an itchy, chronic condition known as Paradigm Rash. Be assured of the following:

- You have plenty of company.

- There is no cure.

If you are over the age of, say, forty-five, you have already seen this New Paradigm (maybe twice), because it's the same one you foisted on your parent's generation twenty years ago (although the clothes and slogans were [slightly] different at the time). Ironically, the hot-blooded proponents of the impending Post-New Paradigm will be completely unaware of this, because of the elimination of American History from the nation's public school curriculum in the early 1970s, during the partial and otherwise unsuccessful implementation of an earlier New Paradigm by the LWEs.[3]

HERE, LET ME HELP YOU—
IT WILL ONLY STING FOR A LITTLE WHILE

Both of these groups are here to help you, to teach you, and to enlighten you. ("Yes, we know you didn't actually *ask* for help— but you're LOST. We can't expect you to recognize your own predicament.")

Since you are about to be "helped," it might be helpful for me to review some important aspects of the helping process (I should acknowledge at this juncture that you didn't ask for *this* help, either. No problem: you can thank me later.) This information will not help you prevent the imminent helping you are about to endure from the Reformer now circling slowly overhead, but it might help you cope with the pain, disorientation and destruction you can expect afterward. Let's have a look:

To be successful,[4] the act of helping requires two crucial components:

- An understanding, by the Helper, of the needs, aspirations and circumstances of the potential Helpee; and,

- Consent from, and participation by, the Helpee.

With extremists, neither of these components is necessary for the commencement of the helping process, which explains their abysmal success rate— and the typical ensuing anger, resentment and bitterness of the Helpee(s). An example might be instructive at this point.

---

3 I was, at least in spirit, a party to this travesty, I'm ashamed to admit.

4 Success, as defined here, is a condition wherein the "helpee" is actually better off than he was before the "helping" began. This condition rarely occurs in the "helping" process.

Imagine I have decided to "help" you by "reorganizing" your garage as a "surprise." Let's analyze the transaction.

Here's what I get out of it:

- Smug satisfaction of helping someone obviously in need;
- Improved self-esteem;
- Your messy garage doesn't bug me anymore;
- A warm feeling of superiority;
- The expectation of your gratitude.

Here's what you get out of it:

- The violation of someone going through all your stuff without your consent;
- Your stuff is now "organized" according to a new system that someone else, who does not have to use the new system, thinks is "logical" and "better";
- Significantly increased difficulty finding anything in your garage;
- The haunting possibility that your "benefactor" threw away something you treasure (which you can't confirm without— you guessed it— reorganizing the garage.);
- The feeling that you owe that person a return "favor";
- A deep welling of homicidal rage.

As we can see, of the two parties involved in the process, only one is better off for the experience and that person, of course, is the Helper. The Helpee's job is to supply (by virtue of his behavior, circumstances, party affiliation, moral weakness, poverty, ethnicity, provincial ignorance or possibly just his mere existence) the raw material for this glorious process.

This "helping" process is the cornerstone of all activism, and the primary source of self-esteem for the activist/practitioner. This need for high self-esteem among activists is the result of deep loathing of some aspect of themselves that would require self-awareness, introspection and painful change to correct. This process looms so awful and difficult in the mind of the activist that ending world hunger or getting teenagers to embrace chastity seems achievable by comparison. Fortunately for the activist, there is a steady, fresh supply of tired, poor, yearning-to-breathe-free people who appear to desperately need intervention and evidently have no need for high self-esteem of their own.

So there's the Helping Process in a nutshell. Now bend over. Don't you feel better already? Call anytime. I'm here for you.

THE TYRANNY OF THE PASSIONATE

Another irritating thing that extremists do is to try to set "Passion Standards" that the rest of us must meet if we would like to participate in the dialogue. The rationalization sounds something like the following, as expressed from the point of view of the extremist:

"I, passionate, caring, aware person:
> volunteer for / belong to / chair; an
> organization / coalition / rant group, and
> write to my congress person / council person / ward boss,
> march on City Hall / the Statehouse / Washington,
> contribute money / time / song writing to, or
> read the newsletter / blog / pamphlet of, and
> revere the celebrities who endorse, the
> movement that is valiantly struggling to,
> begin / end / change / preserve / outlaw / legalize
> (enter Passionately Held Cause here).

If you, my opponent, don't match my:
> enthusiasm / irrationality / shrieking level,
> you're just one more member of the,
> lazy / unenlightened / oblivious masses,

whose complacency / ignorance / greed / immorality,
is the reason for the problem in the first place.

Therefore, your opinion doesn't count."

The idea here is that enthusiasm and activism determine who has credibility in the discourse. So if someone in your world gets all worked up about something that you think ain't broke, you're expected to fight their new cause with equal passion (or volume) if you want a voice in the ensuing debate— which, of course, you aren't interested in having in the first place. In the world of the activist, the medium of exchange is "passion." They've got it, and you don't— game over.

If it happens that this newly minted extremist's bright idea takes a dump on your life in some way— or even if s/he is just plain nuts— then you are compelled to defend yourself by forming your own activist group[5] to protect your (selfish, shallow, unenlightened) interests. Never mind that you've already had to fight off every self-proclaimed visionary who's come along, and you're damned weary of protecting your hard-won little patch of turf. Too bad— put up your dukes.

Ironically, although you have been compelled to join a battle you want nothing to do with, by doing so you instantly become either a self-centered, materialistic conservative or a dangerous, immoral non-believer (depending on the slant of the activist) since you are opposing what is Obviously A Noble Cause.

You might protest at this point that you were just minding your own business. To an activist, "minding your own business" is the worst kind of affront. It demonstrates what an arrogant, self-absorbed, un-observant, callous and shallow person you are, and stokes their passion to reform you to ever-higher levels.

---

5 I, for example, am a founding member of GetOuttaMyFrigginFace.com. Donations, of course, accepted.

KUM BA YAH, ASSHOLE.

Each of these groups holds, as one of its fundamental tenets, some version of a philosophy of Goodwill Toward Others. These tenets are routinely ignored by the members of both groups.

On one hand is the concept of Christian Love. The idea here is that, however scungy, unenlightened, immoral and/or misguided a person is, the Good Christian must extend a hand of loving acceptance to that person. The way Jesus did with the lepers, prostitutes, money-changers and journalists.

History suggests, however, that they have routinely found it more convenient to slaughter "those people" instead of reaching deep inside and finding that loving compassion. Just ask the Moors about Christian Love.[6] These days actual bloodshed is considered less tasteful, so they send modern crusaders like Rush Limbaugh, Glenn Beck and Ann Coulter to protect the Holy Land with the terrible, swift sword of AM radio, denouncing liberal-minded people with an unending stream of invective and ridicule. Jesus must be so proud.

On the other hand, the Progressive Liberal, by exercising the principle of Open-mindedness, is supposed to embrace all peoples, cultures and viewpoints as equally valid and valuable additions to the Glorious Rainbow of Humanity. This principle is enthusiastically followed regarding people who are not white, practice "alternative" anything, espouse bizarre fringe-group manifestos, teach inane tin-foil-hat drivel to our children, hold myopic paranoid world views, propose naïve reform plans, or believe preposterous conspiracy theories. It also applies to everything related to race, gender, class or ethnicity issues of every stripe, but emphatically does not apply to conservative people or their ideas.

Both sides are fixated instead on the annihilation of one another, and dedicate vast amounts of their time, money, manpower (or personpower, depending), and other resources toward this pursuit. The only circumstance that will compel these two groups to honor a truce

---

6 Or the Europeans about Moorish love.

is the arrival of a bunch of Islamist extremists who provide periodic dazzling demonstrations of how to really fuck up an opponent. Only then will our American extremists— realizing they don't have the cubes for Real-Man Opposition— temporarily stand down while the smoking debris is cleared[7] and they can muster enough courage to get back to the silly nit-picking they call a class war.

Despite the avowed core philosophies of each group— Christian Love on the one hand, and Universal Tolerance on the other— there is an inexhaustible supply of anger, invective and hatred available for them to hurl at the other, and many convenient excuses for routinely violating those core philosophies.

Prior to Barack Obama's inauguration, CNN had a panel of commentators giving him a beat-down over his choice of pastor Rick Warren to deliver the invocation at the ceremony. These commentators were the same ones who were dribbling all over themselves during the campaign about the Democratic candidate's rainbow constituency, his message of "inclusiveness," and his plan to heal America's divide— unlike those narrow, elitist Neocons of the Bush Era. Then, suddenly they're ripping the President-elect a new orifice because some right-wing preacher who's against gay marriage is going to get to talk for three minutes in a national forum. Some facts to keep in mind:

- Obama himself is against gay marriage[8].

- Rick Warren wasn't getting a cabinet post: he was just going to say a friggin' prayer.

- The other guy, who was to give the benediction, favors gay marriage. It's called "equal time."

- Obama promised to be the President of ALL Americans, and his supporters in Grant Park cheered wildly at the idea.

- Conservatives are Americans, too.

These commentators— and all the others shrieking about this is-

---

7 Typically by well-funded, efficient capitalist organizations run by white guys.

8 Well, it seems that stance is "evolving."

sue in blogs, chats and coffee-houses— revealed a deep hypocrisy regarding their collective campaign stance about their bold vision for One America:

They didn't really mean it.

Liberals have shown that besides being sore losers, they are also sore winners. They don't just want to have it BOTH ways; they want it ALL ways. I hadn't expected them to reveal the Big Campaign Lie of Inclusiveness quite so soon, but as we have seen many times, they eat their young as soon as they are hatched.

I KNOW WHAT'S BEST FOR YOU: BEND OVER.

Another commonality between these two groups is the conviction that they have a better plan for my life than the one I am currently following.[9] Because they possess "true knowledge," it occurs to them that it is their "duty" to "educate" people like me. Ahh, *Noblesse Oblige*.[10] Never mind that their own lives don't resonate as the shining example of enlightened success that their creeds promise— *I* still need reforming simply because I haven't joined their group yet. In fact, they will never leave me alone until I am converted, cowed, silenced or eliminated.

And it gets worse: If I don't agree with their position, I immediately get labeled as "Part of the problem." You see, it's people like me, with their heads planted securely up their, er… in the sand, who contribute to the problem through apathy and indifference. When confronted with the news of the impending explosion/elimination/degradation/proliferation of whatever-the-fuck, people such as me choose to do nothing, and that's why nothing ever changes/stops/begins/improves.

Of course, the Middle is surrounded by these types, since any dipshit with a laser printer can make himself an official-looking certificate

---

9 I'm not making the case that mine is particularly effective, or better, just that it's— you know— mine.

10 First cloying reference to a classic European text, concept, language, etc. More to come.

that proclaims him an Esteemed Member of a Group that Sees Clearly Into The Future and Must Warn Everyone Else Immediately Before It's Too Late.

Hey, Chicken Little— take a number!

Many members of these groups work hard, contribute money and time to political parties, lobby, protest and proselytize for their agenda, which is, of course, every American's right. The problem for me occurs when their agendas affect my life. Whether they are advocating a return to an agrarian communal utopia or the imposition of fundamentalist moral reforms, what's apparent is that these people have decided that my way of life is either materialistically vapid, decadently perverted or in some other way unacceptable. And they want it changed, NOW.

COUNTERARGUMENT: "Well, Mister Author-Pants, if you're not trying to impose your world view on everyone else, why are you writing this book? — Ha! Gotcha!"

Fair question.[11] The difference is that I'm not contributing to a political party, joining a PAC, calling my congress person, or trying to enact laws that make anyone else do things my way. You can buy my book, or leave it on the shelf. If you do read it, you can write it off as nonsense if you prefer (you won't be the first). I'm offering up some ideas, but no one will be forced to comply with anything presented. The difference is, I'm leaving the choice up to you, and letting you decide how to operate your life.

Besides, I wouldn't have needed to write this book in the first place if you people would leave me the hell alone.[12]

---

11 (Asshole.)

12 This is an example of deflecting/redirecting blame, widely used by politicians and professional victims.

CITIZENS AGAINST CONTINENTAL DRIFT

I have a revenge fantasy about starting a web site for this organization. I figure I could write a few good blog rants, put up a bunch of fake charts, and imply that some government officials were part of a conspiracy. Then I'd get people to pay for "memberships" in my new dot-org, and solicit contributions for the cause. I could be rich.

This could work because people just love to be against stuff, and here in America, we particularly savor being against stuff that can't be changed or isn't going away: like evolution, or racism. Or oppositional politics.

Why do we like to do this so much? I'll explain one reason later under the title: *Long Odds.* Meanwhile, here's another:

Being against something only requires that you point out the flaws and shortcomings of the thing. This can be done while sitting on your ass, sucking on a beer bong and watching porno on cable. It doesn't require that you actually do anything, yet delivers a full portion of self-righteous smugness that you can use to stroke your intellectual/moral woodie. Any fool can point out what's wrong with something.[13] Doing something about it is another story.

CITIZENS AGAINST EVERYTHING

The ultimate expression of this negative philosophy would be another organization I dreamed up: Citizens Against Everything (CAE). Members of this organization would (figuratively, at least) lie down in front of every bulldozer that ever spins its treads. We would be against:

- construction of new buildings;
- demolition of old ones;
- preservation of natural habitat;
- development;
- discrimination;

---

13 For what it's worth, pointing out what's wrong with *everything* is a hell of a lot of work—take it from me.

- affirmative action;
- school reform;
- tenure;
- merit pay;
- No Child Left Behind;
- self-directed learning;
- home schooling;
- government subsidies for food, fuel or commodities;
- high prices for food, fuel, or commodities;
- unions;
- right-to-work legislation;
- job outsourcing;
- third-world sweatshops;
- NAFTA;
- protectionism;
- illegal immigration;
- deportation of illegal immigrants;
- auto company bailouts;
- auto company bankruptcies;
- bank bailouts;
- home foreclosures;
- loan discrimination;
- legislation to prevent loan discrimination...

You get the idea: Everything.

One of the advantages of this type of organization would be high efficiency. Currently, with our two-party system, it takes two enormous groups[14] of people to be against everything, with the burden split pretty much evenly between the two groups. And with each side taking turns, as we do things, there is an appalling waste of resources

---

14 Nearly our entire population, it seems.

as a result. Every four-to-eight years, Party B gets into office and immediately begins canceling all the work previously done by Party A.[15] Then, Party A will work toward getting reelected so they can repeat the process. It's why, in government, nothing much gets done other than widespread and continuous repeal.

Hell, if the idea is to get nothing done, Citizens Against Everything can accomplish that with a hundredth of the workforce, in a fraction of the time, with NO WASTE. In fact, CAE would also eliminate the entire government bureaucracy, except for a few analysts who would periodically issue a report on precisely what hadn't been accomplished during the previous reporting period. Think of the savings.

Of course an organization like this needs a platform:

Platform of Citizens Against Everything

- Dedicated to the proposition that no American should be allowed to get ahead of any other.

- No proposal should be considered if we didn't think of it. The reason we didn't think of it is because we're against proposals.

- We believe we can achieve a national stalemate more efficiently than the two-party system, leaving more budget resources for federal programs— which we would, obviously, oppose.

- We oppose both welfare and corporate welfare, for example. But don't try to enact or abolish either one. We'd oppose that, too.

- If someone has an agenda, we're solidly against it.

A slogan is handy for "branding" purposes, so I've got a couple of those, too:

JOIN TODAY— IT'S THE LAST THING YOU'LL EVER BE "FOR"!™

NO MORE (whatever)!!!™

---

15 In the case of the 2008 election, Obama was texting with his left hand hidden under the Lincoln Bible while taking the oath of office. By the time he arrived in the Oval Office for the first time, his staff had already executed orders to cancel everything that the Bush Administration had ever accomplished (if "accomplish" is, in fact, the correct term).

IDEALISM:
IT ALWAYS SOUNDS LIKE SUCH A GOOD THING.

An ideal is a useful tool for setting activism compass headings. Universal Love, The End of Poverty, No More War, Multicultural Snuggling— all great ideals. The trouble starts when someone thinks the ideal can be achieved. Then they come sniffing around my moral backyard looking for buried bones. Idealists have evidently never heard of the 90/90 rule, used by software coders. It states:

- The first 90% of the job takes 90% of the work;
- The last 10% of the job takes the other 90%.

If you're building a house, it's known as a punch list: a list of small items that will still be unfinished when you eventually sell the place, twenty years later.

Idealists are notoriously bad at the punch list, usually leaving that for the rest of us to finish. When there's a bulldozer that needs lying in front of, you'll have plenty of volunteers. Someone will always be willing to sit in a damn tree for a month if the press attends, but the actual work? That's another story.

THE ENEMY OF THE GOOD.
(Keep trying. So what if it didn't work the last two thousand times?)

There's another thing about us Middles. If something repeatedly fails to work, we'll often try something else. Extremists can't do this, because their belief systems don't allow improvisation. Extremists must follow the required rules, dogmas and rituals, and if they don't achieve success, they're permitted only to redouble their efforts, bolster their faith and try again. Middles, on the other hand, can say to themselves:

> "Well, durn, that's not working. Maybe I'm banging my head against the wall. Guess I'll try something else."

People who seek ideals can never be satisfied, because ideals cannot be realized. Ever. Not even once. But they won't give up. We Middles can see it's never gonna' happen, so we have developed the ability to "settle" for an array of lesser outcomes ranging from "doesn't completely suck," through "pretty darned nice," all the way up to "exceptional"— leaving "perfect" for the extremists to chase until Eternity. The extremists, however, rather than admit they are engaged in a fruitless pursuit, blame someone else— typically their enemies, who they believe are successful only because of the complicity of the amoral/idiot Middles who won't "commit."

DOOMSDAY: THIS TIME IT'S FOR REAL. I MEAN IT.

Everybody thinks they're the canary in the coal mine these days. Stern warnings abound on every subject: food additives, leaching plastic baby bottles, asteroids from space, carbon emissions, bombs in your underpants,[16] "Johnny can't read," sex on TV, sex not on TV, cholesterol, explicit lyrics, moral decline, Wal-Mart, government surveillance, identity theft and another half-million things I'm supposed to worry about. It's getting so bad that it's no longer possible to sit down and enjoy a nice meal of trans fats, alcohol, carbohydrates and artificial coloring— the kind of food that built this great nation, goddammit.

But extremists need Doomsday. It's what they live for. If you consider yourself a member of a special group with a unique vision into impending disaster, you *will* find some impending disasters out there. Then, you'll start trying to scare the shit out of me about it.

---

16 Now, there's a great porn title, if you ask me.

AMERICA: PUT YOUR HEAD BETWEEN YOUR KNEES
AND BREATHE INTO THE BAG.

When I wrote this,[17] President Bush had just signed the *Appallingly Ginormous Bailout Act of 2008*, which would either:

- Restore the Economy and Prevent the Total Collapse of Civilization As We Know It, or,
- Be a Colossal, Pointless Waste of Money, Resulting in the Total Collapse of Civilization As We Know It.
- Or possibly something else.[18] [19]

Americans seem to have lost the ability to take a deep breath. We take our temperature every 2.3 minutes by tuning in to CNN (or Fox), logging online, checking our podcasts, our Twitter feeds[20] or some way or another plugging in to see what's going on "out there."

One of the problems with "out there" is that the journalists, commentators, politicians, bloggers, soothsayers and everyone else who is a source of news, information or hogwash has a vested interest in jacking up the Fear Factor.

Flip on the TV and check out your favorite network's current news team: Chicken Little (the babe with big hair) and Chicken Littler (the old guy), who will be busily "Leading with the Bleeding" news of the Meltdown *du Jour.* One month it was gas prices, and the news feeds were full of scary stories of impending lines and shortages. They trotted out "average-guy/gal" interviews with nimrods that predicted that

---

17 By now, it should be obvious that this book was not written in a "linear" fashion. It is probably also obvious that it is, in fact, a bunch of unrelated "rant-ettes," poorly stitched together into a dubious narrative. Aren't we glad we "democratized" publishing?

18 Neither, as it turns out. Since I wrote this section, President Obama has deemed it necessary to propose the *Appallingly Ginormous-er Bailout Act of 2009*, which will either: (see above).

19 Getting a book written takes forever, it seems. Since I wrote that last footnote, President Obama has signed the "*Let's Rebuild America By Putting Signs On Every Highway In America Announcing A Recovery Act Project*" *Act of 2010*, which will either: — you get the idea.

20 What do vacuous, horny 19-year-olds think about the current foreign-policy situation? Jeepers, don't forget to check your Tweets!

they would lose their jobs because they couldn't afford to drive to work.

—Please. Does anybody think about this shit before they broadcast it? Does anyone run the damned numbers first? Well, I did.

Let's say you commute 30 miles to work, and you have a car that gets 22 MPG/city. Gas just jumped a buck a gallon. Run the numbers, for Crissake: that's 300 miles a week, divided by 22 MPG. That means you need less than 14 gallons of gas for the week's commute, which costs you $14 more than it did last week. We're supposed to believe that this asshole's family financial plan is going to be dashed upon the jagged rocks of bankruptcy due to a $14 weekly cost increase? That's three lattés![21]

Never mind that the decreased fuel consumption by all these panicky Americans caused the Arabs to bend to the immutable laws of supply and demand, resulting in record price drops at the pump within the month. Down to a buck-fifty in my neck of the woods. Made for good copy, though.

BLURTOSIS

Lisa was traveling by air about one month before the 2008 Presidential election. As she was boarding the plane, and just starting to get settled in her seat, the passenger next to her— a complete stranger— asks:

"Who are you going to vote for?"

Now, to some of us archaic folk, that is tantamount to asking to see our most recent bank statement, or saying:

"Excuse me, is that psoriasis or eczema?"

The correct answer to this type of intrusive question is something akin to:

"You are a complete stranger, asking me personal questions while I am trying to buckle my seat belt low and snug across

---

21 Or a 12-pack of Bud Light, 2 decent microbrews or good start on a twenty sack.

my lap according to instructions delivered by some mincing-
ly gay flight attendant on a commercial airliner. Perhaps you
should consider 'deplaning' so you can find a quiet corner in
the airport where you can go fuck yourself."

Alas, one seldom has the presence of mind to deliver such a tart
rejoinder in these situations. So she said:

"Actually, I'm undecided."

An Undecided Voter. Might as well have been a quadriplegic tore-
ador in a bright-red wheelchair. The woman pounced immediately:

"OmigodyouvejustgottovoteforBarakObamahestheonlycan-
didatewhocansavetheplanetfeedthehungrystopthegreedycor-
poratefatcatsfromrobbingusallandsendingourjobsoverseas-
whilerestoringtheeconomytotheglorythatisoncewasduringth-
eClintonadministrationbeforeGeorgeWBushandhisevilHal-
libutonlovingcroniesgotusinthemosthorriblewarinhistory-
aslongasyoudontincludeanyhistoryfartherbackthansay1980
(pant, pant, pant!)."

Well. What are you supposed to say to that?

"Thank you very much, uh— what's your name, again?— for
pointing out what an uninformed asshole I am. Perhaps I
should have considered engaging in activities such as watching
television, reading books, magazines or newspapers, surfing the
web or talking to other people so I could be informed enough
to have decided already. This should be a very enlightening couple of hours ahead of us. Perhaps you can point out some of my
character flaws and personality shortcomings while we're at it.
That way, when I arrive at my destination, I can cancel all my
plans and devote myself to being more like you."

The woman in the adjacent seat was suffering from a curious condition known as Blurtosis— similar to a mild form of Tourette's Syn-

drome. Blurtosis manifests itself in activists and other True Believers as the inability to censor one's self in situations where the rules of civil behavior suggest that one ought to shut-the-fuck-up. The syndrome occurs because the sufferer is so hyper focused on his or her pet issue, and has been ruminating on it all day/week/month/eon, that it has become impossible to contain it when an unsuspecting victim accidentally provides an opportunity for the sufferer to vent. It's like popping a champagne cork.

It works something like this:

Middle: "Good morning!"

Blurtosis sufferer: "Well, it would be if George Bush and his larcenous band of NeoCons weren't busy destroying the country and making us the laughingstock of the entire world!"

Middle, muttering to self: ("Shit. Maybe I can fake a *Grand Mal* seizure.")

Or in the other version:

Middle: "Good morning!"

Blurtosis sufferer: "Yes, it is, because of the Good Lord's blessings. Have you accepted Jesus Christ as your personal savior?"

Middle, muttering to self: ("Aw, Jezus. Not one of these, again. And what's a 'personal savior' anyway? As opposed to a 'timeshare' savior?")

Or, since the 2008 election, the newest version:

Middle: "Good morning!"

Blurtosis sufferer: "Well it might be temporarily, but don't get used to it. At this exact moment, Obama is secretly transforming the Greatest Country On Earth into the world's first Muslim Marxist tyranny. And he's doing it by shipping trainloads of illegal Mexicans right through Arizona and giving them citizenship at secret locations in California if they promise to be Democrats. Then he's going to give them all my guns."

Middle, muttering to self: ("Geez. Wasn't eight years of this kind of bullshit enough?")

Blurtosis occurs because the activist/true believer is undergoing a crisis of faith.[22] For the LWE, this occurs every four years. Depending on the outcome of the election, the condition will persist in one of two forms until the next one. In the first form, Blurtosis manifests itself as an unending series of complaints and I-told-you-so remarks, in which every bad thing that happens anywhere is blamed on the current administration. In the other form, it manifests itself as an unending series of "observations" about how every good thing that happens anywhere is attributable to the current administration, and every bad thing is the result of interference by the other party.

For the RWE, the condition persists pretty much as it has for the last 2,000 years or so, manifested by the irrepressible desire to share the Glory of God's Love, and is not affected by current events, social change, human progress, overwhelming science or anything else.

Now, with the Tea Party/Hatriot movement in full rant, we can add Health Care, Socialism, guns, Muslim-paranoia, God, Country, the flag and "Oh, what the hell— let's challenge Obama's citizenship!" into the mix.

Lisa's personal savior on the plane? iPod. She put in the earbuds and made it clear to the Blurtosoid in the next seat that she wasn't available as a lecture victim.

---

22 Faith is permanently in crisis, because it requires that you steadfastly believe something that is endlessly under attack by doubt, reason, facts, fear and other threats.

BUT, ENOUGH ABOUT ME.
WHAT DO YOU THINK ABOUT ME?

Because of the combined effects of Idealism, hyper excitability and Blurtosis, personal relationships with activists/true believers eventually take on an asymmetrical quality. What once might have been a mutually beneficial relationship (friend, lover, spouse, coworker, neighbor) devolves into a lopsided one similar to Mentor/Protégé, or worse, Interrogator/Detainee. Regardless of severity, the altered relationship is involuntary on the part of the protégé, who is held hostage by his desire to preserve the balanced, bilateral relationship that once was.

How irritating can this get? Let's imagine that you are currently writing a book of... oh... let me see... how about this? — Political Commentary. Hypothetical situation. You have been working on the book for quite some time, thinking about the subject continually, and are convinced that you have a unique and fresh viewpoint that is going to go viral if you can just get the thing finished and in print.

You might find yourself saying things like:

> "Interesting point, Stan. That very subject is covered brilliantly in my book— did you know I was writing a book? No? Well, it's a biting and witty commentary about how utterly full of shit everyone else is, unless they see things precisely the way I do (I'll give you a discount once it's out because I have NO DOUBT an intelligent person like yourself will completely agree with my every glimmering insight). Meanwhile, I *could* give you a little peek inside. What? Oh, no problem— this will only take a minute. No, really, I've got time. This part is really funny— I laugh at it every time I read it. OK, here's the setup ..."

In this— again, entirely hypothetical— situation, you might start to notice people rolling their eyes, exchanging frightened glances, suddenly coming down with terminal diseases or moving to Maine and leaving no forwarding address.

People are doing this for several reasons:

- They've already heard about your fucking book;
- They haven't noticed any evidence that you are more intelligent, observant, witty, wise or better off in any way than themselves;
- They didn't ask for your viewpoint;
- You are not an expert on any subjects presented in your book;
- You never listen to them explain their pet philosophy *ad nauseum*; in fact, you don't appear to have one *iota* of interest in anything about them.

This is what it's like to be in a relationship with an extremist. It's the human-interaction equivalent of waterboarding.

DID YOU GET ALL THAT?

You're paying attention, aren't you? This is important, goddammit! All right then— I thought you were drifting off there for a minute…

Moving on.

Part Two:

BELIEF SYSTEMS

Another commonality of these two groups is their use of belief systems as tools for ensuring individual loyalty, team spirit, and group solidarity. Belief systems help the practitioner to cling tightly to a philosophy in the face of torrents of contradictory information and threatening, nagging doubt.

Liberals are going to object strenuously to the assertion that they employ anything remotely resembling a belief system, because the abolition of belief systems is a cornerstone of progressive philosophy. Progressive Liberalism is— they will remind us— based on scientific principles, in which all "facts" are provisional, waiting expectantly to be overturned by new evidence. How, then, does one explain the paradigm-shattering changes that have taken place in various realms of our society such as the sciences, communications, medicine, psychology and just about everything else, while Progressive Liberalism has remained essentially unmodified since at least the mid-1960's?[1] There are still Hippies, for Crissake! Didn't they get the memo that explained it was all just an embarrassing fad?

One significant flaw in all belief systems is that they require constant reinforcement for the believer, because the system is under constant assault by contradictory— or at minimum, ambiguous— information. Because it is impossible for the believer to prove that his world view is correct, the best way to feel better about "betting the bank" on that world view is to get other people (as many as possible) to believe it, too. Consequently, proselytizing and recruiting are essential to activism, and great effort is applied to these pursuits.

All of this effort satisfies only temporarily, though, owing to the unending assault by doubt, contradiction and temptation upon the walls of the philosophical fort. Redoubling of proselytigical[2] zeal is the result, and it is typically directed at the rest of us.

Let us explore some common belief mechanisms utilized by extremists:

---

1 The 1920's, more accurately.

2 No, it's not in the dictionary.

CONSPIRACY!
(Just because you can't *prove* it isn't true
doesn't mean it *isn't,* isn't true.)

Huh?

One common trait of extremists/believers is that they have some type of itch that can't be scratched. It might be social injustice, gender inequality, impending socialism, states' rights or the thought of other people having recreational sex. Maybe watching the polar ice caps disappear troubles them. Regardless of what it is that bugs the activist, nothing bugs her/him more than the fact that:

NOTHING SEEMS TO BE HAPPENING TO STOP IT.[3]

There is a host of possible reasons for this, *all* which the extremist refuses to consider:

- No one else gives a shit;
- No one is in charge of doing something about it;
- His Big Idea has already been tried unsuccessfully— perhaps many times;
- He really sucks at getting The Word out, so no one knows about it;
- People are working on it, but it can't be done as fast as he would like;
- People are working on it, but he doesn't know this because he immerses himself in biased, paranoid, ill-informed bullshit that reinforces his incorrect opinion:
- It can't be fixed, period;
- It *shouldn't* be "fixed";

---

3 Or start it, prevent it, enable it, sanction it, legalize it, or etcetera-ize it.

- Everyone is working on other problems;
- His Big Idea is wrong;
- He is a wacko.

Activists/believers will NEVER consider any of these possibilities. As a result, intense frustration accompanies their efforts to Change The World— primarily because The World will not listen to them. Nothing is more irritating to them than feeling that they got screwed/impeded/quashed/negated/ignored and not being able to identify who did it to them. For Extremists, the Conspiracy is a handy tool that performs several important jobs:

- It allows them to feel victimized by some big, scary monster;
- It allows them to rationalize inaction because the conspirators are too powerful, too secretive or too organized;
- It reinforces their special status as a Believer, because the Truth of their beliefs is so profoundly frightening to Others that the Others must rally together to suppress them through complex, secret activities;
- It allows them to ignore all the possibilities on the previous list, and in particular, the "wacko" part.

Here are a few potential explanations to consider if you are an extremist and you find yourself feeling that everyone is screwing you because *they* can't handle the Truth:

- You got screwed and somebody got away with it;
- You got screwed by random circumstances, and nobody "did it" to you;
- You screwed yourself and are unaware of it;
- You screwed yourself and don't want to face it;
- You feel screwed because your expectations are unreasonable;
- Nothing whatsoever happened to you, but you are addicted to victimhood;

- You deserved it;
- There was a conspiracy.

Let's explore that last item, The Conspiracy. In addition to the allure of the convenient mental mechanisms that come with being a victim of a conspiracy, there's another, much more important reason that extremists so readily believe in these theories: The extremists typically belong to the kind of group that has the attributes necessary to conceive, organize, and successfully pull off a conspiracy, so it seems entirely plausible to them that others are capable of doing it, too. These attributes include:

- A strongly held belief system;
- Intense emotional underpinnings supporting the belief system;
- Shared goals;
- Rigid doctrine;
- A hierarchical command structure (typically with a charismatic, dictatorial leader);
- Common enemies;
- A shared desire to destroy those enemies;
- An isolating peer group (see Cloistering, part 4, Operational Methodologies);
- Heightened fear, suspicion and feelings of victimhood;
- Copious free time.

Because the True Believer occupies a tightly closed, self-referential community that wishes to impose its world view on everyone else (or destroy them if unsuccessful), s/he assumes that everyone else is in a similar community and is occupied with trying to do some imposing/ destroying back in the other direction. Occasionally this is true, but more often not. It is inconceivable to a worked-up Believer that the world is not against him,[4] or worse— completely disinterested, as is more often the case.

On the other hand, the groups that are typically *accused* of being perpetrators of conspiracies (Big Business, Big Government, Secret Marxist Cabals, Law Enforcement, The Man) are probably the ones least likely to be pulling them off, precisely because they lack the unifying attributes listed previously. Big Business, for example, is not the type of unified group with the shared purposes required to successfully pull off a conspiracy of any meaningful sort.

I'm not saying that it never happens. But I think it's much more likely that the parties in these institutions are too self-interested to get involved in something as risky— and with such poor chances of success— as a conspiracy, especially when they have a simpler, legal alternative: they can just gouge you at the pump or cash register. Besides, they don't like sharing with one other, and conspirators must be willing to share.

These larger groups are not united under a charismatic, dogmatic leadership (there's no Louis Farrakhan of the business world, for example. Not even Jack Welch had that kind of charisma) that can or does command the obedience of the others in the group. A typical CEO can't terrorize or brainwash the organization's employees into some communal illegal act. Hell, he can't fire someone in less than about two years, and not without significant documentation. How can someone so hamstrung turn enough people into mindless Corporate Commandos in order to pull of a conspiracy? Anyone who believes this is possible has never worked for a large organization.

Not only that, but everyone in the top third of the organizational chart wants the CEO's job, and will rat him out in a minute if given the chance. Busting the CEO's conspiracy-in-the-making would be an irresistible upward career move.

Nevertheless, here's how all this is supposed to happen, according to Conspiracy Theory:

---

4 Actually, that's part of the appeal.

A group of highly competitive people (mostly white men) agree— on extremely short notice— to engage in a probably unnecessary conspiracy in which EVERYONE stops backbiting, cajoling, jockeying and undermining, while simultaneously suspending their well-honed talents for sneakiness, obfuscation, jealousy, greed, insubordination and general disrespect for authority (including that of the new conspiracy's leadership), while also simultaneously organizing a new, untested command structure based on risky unethical and/or criminal activity, while also, also simultaneously endorsing an action plan without personal input or committee oversight, while also, also, also simultaneously adopting a compensation package to divide the spoils. And if they get caught, they will all go to prison except the leaders.

Not likely. For that kind of activity, you need a Religion or a Cause.

Rather, the most-likely outcomes of a conspiracy by one of these non charismatic groups are as follows, ranked by decreasing likelihood:

- Failure;
- Discovery;
- Failure and subsequent discovery;
- Discovery, then failure;
- Dissolution because of infighting;
- Revolt by a group of co-conspirators who are unhappy with pay scale and/or benefits package;
- Dissipation through lack of resources;
- Squabbling over titles, followed by dissolution;
- Sub-conspiracy by smaller group of Young-Turk conspirators;
- Stalemate among competing subgroups of Young Turks;
- Dissolution due to unexpected availability of tee time at a prestigious Country Club;
- Ratting-out by undercover agent;

- Exposure by underappreciated, underpaid-for-the-same-work female "slut-with-a-heart-of-gold" whistle-blower who is the Only Person in the Organization with a Conscience (because she is a single mother);

- Success.

One commonly expressed conspiracy theory involves the Fat Cats from the oil and automotive industries colluding to sell us gas-guzzling SUVs that must be nursed with ever-higher-priced fuel. This is a magnificent example of a situation that does not need a conspiracy to work. Given the following facts, which of the oil and/or automotive companies' Evil Goals cannot be met without a time-consuming, risky, illegal conspiracy?

Facts:

- *Americans will drive gas-guzzling vehicles— capable of carrying seven passengers but transporting only two— while towing trailers laden with other gas-guzzling vehicles such as snowmobiles, ATVs, boats and motorcycles, to the beach, forest, lake, motocross track or mountains, where they will park the SUVs and start up the ancillary vehicles to take turns riding in/on them for fun while destroying the environment and disturbing the peace.*

- *All the vehicles described above will be made of petrochemicals and other materials that require massive energy expenditures to produce and must be imported from around the world in fuel-consuming ships, trains and planes.*

- *En route, these folks will roar past a few low-powered hybrid vehicles, snickering at the fools therein.*

- *All 17 cup holders will contain a one-use, PET water bottle that will be thrown in the waste stream. These bottles will use petroleum in their manufacture, transportation and disposal.*

- *At other times they will leave their vehicles idling while they pick up the dry cleaning, kids, dog, single-use bottled water, etc.*

- *They will do these things despite the current price of gasoline, however high it might be, while grumbling about government inaction.*

- *They will happily pay $6 per gallon for bottled spring water, $17 for 750ml of Shiraz and $3.75 for a 12-ounce cup of coffee.*[5]

No one is forcing them to do this, and they are not benumbed drones in the thrall of some conspiratorial mind-control scheme by a Detroit-Riyadh cabal. They are driving oversized, fuel-slurping vehicles because they are Americans, they can afford it, and they just don't give a shit.

So Big Oil and Big Auto don't need a conspiracy. They don't need to know one another. All they need to do is make the SUVs, put a gas station on every tenth corner, and we will do the rest.

No conspiracy. So sorry. People just can't accept the idea that just because something can't be explained doesn't mean there's a cover-up. Sometimes the killer gets away with it, the crop circles are a hoax, the lights can't be identified and nothing sinister is going on behind the barbed wire.

JUST A THOUGHT …

Conspiracy theories thrive on a paucity of evidence— in fact, the less evidence the better. Accordingly, one has to wonder if religion is the biggest conspiracy theory of them all. *Think* about it:

- IMMENSELY powerful and secretive forces are at play;

- It's rife with unanswered, unanswerable questions;

- There is no evidence whatsoever that any of it is true or actually happened;

- Faith, rather than quashed, is bolstered by the lack of evidence;

---

5 Even at $2.25 per gallon, gasoline is one of the better deals we can get for any liquid we consume in this country.

- The more you look into it, the more ambiguous it becomes;
- What's with all those robes? What's going on under there?

PSEUDOSCIENCE: FAITH DISGUISED.

Maybe someone can explain to me how a person can simultaneously denounce religion and embrace astrology, or vice versa. Both involve unseen forces emanating from the Heavens, and both attempt to provide complex explanations for simple things whose meaning is quite obvious to others. Both systems provide murky, convoluted reasoning that can be applied to any situation in which "shit" has "happened." And both systems rely on a select group of people who represent themselves as possessors of special insight that qualifies them to provide guidance and clarity for understanding the unknowable and unseen.

Yet they seem to be mutually exclusive groups. You won't find many Astrolo-Christians out there, for example. Astrology and other pseudosciences such as numerology, rebirthing, Scientology, Primal Therapy and homeopathy seem to me to have some commonalities:

First, they appear to me to be widely embraced by people who are uncomfortable with traditional Abrahamic belief systems. Often these people also hold themselves to be members of the intellectual elite— which is, in part, why they "can't" be religious. Others, I suspect, don't like all the moral rules that accompany the theology (you can put me in this category, although that does not mean I'm a perv. Necessarily). Some have been buggered by priests.

Second, they seem to use two basic techniques:

- Explaining simple questions with unnecessarily complex answers, and,
- Explaining complex questions with dangerously oversimplified answers.

Many, many people seem deeply uncomfortable with the idea that life is a slow, plodding odyssey, racked with suffering and struggle, rife with doubt and uncertainty, after which you die and, before long, no one remembers you or gives a shit about anything you did while you were here. If you happen to be one of these uncomfortable people, *and* you've preemptively rejected conventional religions for one reason or another, you may find yourself aching for a way to fill a "spiritual void." That's where pseudoscience, New-Age spirituality, clueless adoption of Eastern philosophies, the resurgence of primitive religions like Wicca and Paganism— and most-recently— the Democratic Party, come in.

ALL TOGETHER NOW.

About a month before the 2008 election, an e-mail went around with a link to an appalling YouTube video showing a group of children singing a song extolling how "Obama's gonna' change the world." The director of this chorus was an eager young woman who was evidently quite proud of her accomplishment and was jumping around encouraging her young charges to sing with great vigor. In the background were beaming parents and other adults playing musical instruments to accompany the singers. However, if you turned off the audio, you would swear it was a video taken during Bible Study. Or a classroom in North Korea.[6]

Now, I have no doubt these parents had good intentions, and who *wouldn't* want their children to celebrate the coming New Era of Universal Love, Cross-Cultural/Color-Blind/Gender-Neutral Equality, and Boundless Wellspring of Realized Human Potential? — Fuckin' Age of Aquarius, Dude!

Except for one problem: If a public schoolteacher tried to get the kids to sing "Jesus Loves Me, This I Know, Etc." a Supreme Court case would have been filed before the last strains of the innocent young voices echoed off the walls of the building. The hypocrisy of the moment did not go unnoticed by the World Wide React-O-Sphere.

---

6 Given the exactly politically correct demographic mixture of children in the video, it is unlikely that it could be mistaken for North Korea. Nevertheless, the analogy is still valid.

Appropriately, within hours of the posting, satiric versions had appeared on YouTube as well, with visuals of North Korean children and Hitler Youth singing to the Obama sound track. Which demonstrates two important points:

- There are many people who saw this stunt as the disgusting, vile, Airstrip One-style mind control attempt that it was, and,

- There are many people who have nothing important to do all day but produce unpaid, satiric videos.

Notwithstanding the nauseating spectacle of these parents happily pimping their children for a political cause the kids couldn't possibly comprehend and shouldn't be a part of, the glaring similarity to religious indoctrination was inescapable to me. Which got me wondering (what doesn't? you're probably asking yourself).

PROGRESSIVE LIBERALISM: OUR NEWEST RELIGION

What are some distinguishing features of a religion? Perhaps foremost is a Body of Doctrine. These are the concepts, rules and texts that must be accepted by the True Believers without question or criticism. We're all familiar to some degree with the doctrine of fundamentalist religions:

- God's Word as written in our Holy Book is the only truth;

- Heaven awaits only the righteous;

- Damnation awaits the sinner;

- Women are subordinate;

- Sex is naughty;

- Our religion is caring, merciful, and forgiving;

- Other religions are corrupt, misguided, and wrong,

- Nevertheless, we are tolerant of others' beliefs (yeah, right).

- We look serious and important in these funny hats.

The extreme (and to some extent the not-so-extreme) Left has its body of doctrine as well, and true believers have been repeating these mantras for so long that they have become the Unassailable Truths of the Progressive Liberal Doctrine. As a Progressive Liberal, you are not permitted to question these tenets. Some examples:

- Capitalism = Greed;
- Liberals are the only people who care about the Earth;
- Republicans are warmongers who have gotten us into most of our nation's armed conflicts (for a real surprise, look this up);
- The Democratic Party has a stunningly successful legislative, foreign policy, leadership and reform track record;
- Corruption is a uniquely conservative/capitalistic phenomenon;
- Drug companies are evil institutions dedicated to screwing poor people;
- All problems can be solved through intellect;
- There is something inherently dignified about being poor (unless you are poor and white);
- Rich people don't work hard or deserve what they possess;
- Hate speech should be considered equivalent to physical violence;
- The United States is the most aggressive, exploitative warmongering country in the world;
- Terrorist attacks are "payback" for flawed America foreign policy;
- Everyone deserves to have high self-esteem;
- Hemp is useful for something.

Many more liberal dogmatic "truths" prevail, regarding a wide range of subjects such as nuclear power, the World Bank/globalization, stolen elections, victimhood, gender issues, and diversity.

My point is not that this collection of views is necessarily ground-less. Much of it is based on real issues— or issues that were real in 1964, but no longer— that have devolved into stereotype, dogma, and hyperbole.

The point is that questioning this doctrine is heresy. Even if parts of the doctrine are demonstrably false— speech does not equal violence, and no, not everyone deserves to have high self-esteem—[7] questioning the doctrine will get you hammered every bit as hard as challenging a fundamentalist about Creation Science.

Another religious feature of PL is the intense peer pressure to con-form. You are supposed to accept the entire doctrine, repeat the man-tras, attend the demonstrations, love the music (example: you cannot be a PL and dislike Bono), oppose all war, revise history, vote for what-ever jerk the Democratic Party scrapes up, pretend there is a govern-ment conspiracy against hemp, and take seriously Arianna Huffington and other Gulfstream Liberals.

Extreme intolerance of other points of view is yet a third "religious" behavior practiced by liberals. Just as fundamentalists will dismiss crit-ics and others who don't See The Light as "sinners," the Left has taken to labeling all conservatives, undecideds and anyone else who doesn't agree with them as "red-state idiots." Keep in mind: this is the party of intellectuals. All those diplomas, yet by late 2008, the sophistication level of public debate coming from the Left had been reduced to this:

- "Bush is an Idiot."
- "Anyone who supports Bush[8] is an Idiot."
- "Anyone who doesn't join us in denouncing Bush is an Idiot."
- "Anyone who objects to flawed logic used in the criticism of Bush is an Idiot."
- "Anyone in the same party as Bush is an Idiot."

---

7 Assholes, for example. Why should they deserve to have high self-esteem?

8 Since this book was started, "Teabaggers" has replaced "Red-State Idiot" as the LWE shorthand designation for conservatives.

Fourth graders can mount a more cogent argument than that (assuming they attend private school).

This type of absolutist reasoning is a significant feature of religious thought. You may recognize this style of thinking in such utterances as:

- "He who does not worship Allah is an infidel."
- "He who does not accept Jesus Christ will go to Hell."
- "Oy, gevalt! You vant to marry a shiksa?"

"DUDE, HAND ME THAT CLAY TABLET."

However, Progressive Liberalism did not morph into a religion overnight. In fact, the process had been moving rather slowly over the past few decades until two pivotal events occurred. The first was the election[9] of George W. Bush to the Presidency in the year 2000. Dubya's ascent to the office provided the budding Progressive Liberal proto-religion with a much-needed feature: The Perfect Satan.

With Bush, the LWEs had someone to blame for everything that they didn't like about, well ... everything. And blame they did, with vengeance and ardor unseen in recent political history, the Nixon years inclusive. They would blame Bush and/or his puppet-master Neocons for: global warming; inflation; recession; joblessness; illegal immigration; abuses against said illegal immigrants, declining wages; rising ocean levels; disappearing rain forests; high gas prices; low self-esteem; all previous, current and future wars; the pissy attitude of the French and other preening Euro-trash critics; terrorism itself and the failure to predict/prevent/foresee/forestall it; racial discrimination; drug abuse; gender inequity; school violence; job outsourcing; AIDS; failed banks; teen pregnancy; genital mutilation, why-Johnny-can't-read; species eradication; chromosomal mutation; global loss of respect; colorectal cancer; postnasal drip; jock itch; voter ennui; and anything and everything else that is broken, irritating, unfair, fails to live up to irrational

---

9 Hanging Chads! He's stealing the election! Did you see that?

expectations, doesn't sit right with someone or just ain't fittin'.[10]

Bush-as-Satan provided Liberals with the convenient Black/White, Good/Evil mental shorthand that religious followers have enjoyed for millennia— and permission to dispense with the messy, time-consuming process of data collection, analysis, further inquiry, hypothesis formation, testing and evaluation that leads one to those prized scientific, provisional understandings of the highly complex, multipart, long-term processes behind such things as global economics, international politics, climate systems, the human condition and other big issues that governments and their leaders are tasked with managing.

With George Bush, blame for EVERYTHING could be efficiently assigned with a single, quick, bold-stroke utterance: "George Bush and his fucking Neocons."

Now, before you get all lathered up that I'm some sort of Bush sycophant, keep this in mind: I didn't vote for the guy, and no, I wasn't impressed with him as President. But when I objected to lapses in logic during people's irrational anti-Bush political ranting, I routinely got labeled as some sort of conservative apologist. When I made these objections, I wasn't defending Bush, Cheney or any of those guys. I was defending logic and reason from irrational, emotional assaults by people who should know better than to engage in that kind of shit. In fact, the affliction was eventually given a name: Bush Derangement Syndrome (BDS).[11]

Liberals are people who claim to stand for intellect, reason, scientific process, education, literacy, fairness, equality, objectivity, skepticism and openness, among other things, but when faced with a powerful administration that has a different world view, they behave just like those they criticize for lacking these same qualities.

In other words, like religious zealots.

---

10 Never mind that Dubya was also supposed to be the singular Presidential dumb-ass of all time. Here's a question: If you get taken by a dumb-ass, what does that make you?

11 This has since been supplanted by Obama Derangement Syndrome and Palin Derangement Syndrome.

Anyhow, with the arrival of a Political Satan, Progressive Liberalism was poised to become a fully fledged religion. Only one thing was missing:

A Messiah.

Enter Barack Obama, stage left.[12]

Born of the perfect Liberal Mary and Joseph: a nice white girl from the Midwest and a black, Muslim intellectual from Kenya, Little Lord Barack was raised in a transnational, cross-cultural, broken home where through the process of witnessing inequality, suffering and strife, he learned to care about the downtrodden and the unfortunate. Seeing misery and injustice all around him, he traveled to the Temple of Ivy League to learn more. Then, after Filling the Cup of Knowledge, he departed for the Sodom and Gomorrah of Politics: the Chicago 'hood,' where he raised the lame, invigorated the spent, unwretched the wretched masses, and emerged miraculously unsoiled from the morass of the most-corrupt political environment in our country while decrying the sins of the Capitalist Money-Changers (and amassing $700 million in the process).[13] Harnessing the power of hellfire oratory, he compelled The People to rise up against Pontius Bush and the Clinton Pharisees, and when The People were gathered, Barrack slew the Lion of Injustice with Martin Luther King's jawbone and Rent the Temple of Conservatism unto a pile of smoldering rubble. And The People texted that they were Pleased.[14]

By this moment in history, every soul on Earth had seen the now-iconic image of Obama looking Heavenward in a Jesus Christ-meets-Vladimir Lenin pose of Serene Inner Peace, Hope for the Future, and

---

12 Well, barely left of center stage, it turns out. Unless you ask someone with Obama Derangement Syndrome.

13 Stealing the election is heinous. Buying it, apparently, is acceptable.

14 OK, I admit that got a bit out of hand— not to mention the obvious convolution of Biblical texts. But when a writer (particularly a novice) produces a phrase such as "slew the Lion of Injustice with Martin Luther King's jawbone," it's impossible not to use it.

Equality for the Proletariat.[15] In one election season, that image had been seen by more people than have collectively gazed upon the previous Leftist Political Iconography record-holder: that utterly irritating image of Che Guevara wearing his fucking "Beret of Justice." Consequently, I'm torn: on the one hand, the possibility that Che's hyper exploited image might finally be put to rest fills me with hope (the audacity!), but on the other, its replacement by THE OBAMA IMAGE fills me with dread.

Here in Denver, art galleries were fronting shows with images of Obama's face morphing into that of Abraham Lincoln, Martin Luther King or John F. Kennedy. Scores of glassy-eyed politicos gathered 'round and swooned over the Deep Significance of the juxtaposition of Obama's visage with that of the guy who freed the slaves, the guy who died for the cause of racial equality, or the guy who doinked Marilyn Monroe. Excuse me, but Obama hadn't DONE ANYTHING YET. (Well, OK, he had proved the efficacy of web-based social networking as a highly effective marketing medium, and shown that outspending your opponent five-to-one will get you a four percent lead in the election results— as long as your opponent has one foot in the grave and/ or screws up every political opportunity she or he gets.)

But as of the election, he hadn't freed any slaves.[16] So before we raise him to the status of a Lincoln, King, or Barrack of Nazareth, shouldn't we wait until he actually *does* something?[17]

After the inauguration, I wished him well (not in person,) and hoped that he would do great things for our country, but it seems to me that we're denigrating our real heroes by anointing people who just look as if they might do great things. Remember, the guy has hardly any track record. Next, we'll see his face on our fucking currency.

---

15 Plagiarized, it seems. Am I the only one who finds it odd that, as much as Liberal young people revere artists, they have no compunction about stealing their work?

16 Still hadn't, as of the 2010 mid-terms.

17 Evidently not. Since I wrote this, the Nobel committee gave him the Peace Prize for "being a beacon of hope" or some blather like that. Some of the previous recipients melted down their medals to make letter openers.

Anyway, now the Liberals had their Messiah, and they had already started crediting him with Saving the World. When I wrote this section, he was not yet sworn in, yet people were yammering about how he had Made It Possible To Be Proud To Be An American Again;[18] how he was going to Rescue the Economy with his Loaves and Fishes Stimulus Plan for several million Green Jobs; and how he was going to "Rebrand America."

Rebrand America? What the fuck? Are these really the same people who think that the world hates us because we are a morass of shallow, mass-marketed commercial drivel that is polluting everyone and everything with a vile slurry of Wendy's Baconator wrappers and empty Starbucks cups? So the Democratic Party had become an organization dedicated to big-budget political hyperbranding, had it? To hell with all those downtrodden underdogs.

—Well.

It appears that I'm off subject.   Again.

Let's summarize briefly. Here's what the various religions have in common:

- Unchallengeable dogma

- Intolerance of dissent

- Tunnel vision

- Self-anointed righteousness

- Self-appointed authority

- Charismatic leadership

- Emotional involvement by the rank-and-file.

---

18 Just curious— is that how you guys see all your relationships? Loyalty only during the good times? For Better but not Worse, Richer but not Poorer? Americans have plenty to be proud of— contributions by both parties— that should be enough to get us through the rough spots. I didn't renounce my country when friggin' Carter was in the White House.

- Moral certitude
- Disdain for the unwashed
- Disrespect for other viewpoints
- Abysmal success record
- Resistance to self-examination
- Resistance to change[19]
- Deeply rooted hypocrisy

Here's where they differ:

- Views on sex, drugs and rock n' roll
- Operational specifics regarding the running of *my* life

PROGRESSIVE LIBERALISM IS A RELIGION?
—LORD HELP US.

How did this happen? I'll explain it all in a moment, but first, allow me to present my credentials as a Social Scientist:

- _____

Okay, I admit that's not an impressive display, but *real* intellectuals don't need credentials to hold forth on any subject of their choosing, so why do I? I can claim only to have— to paraphrase Yogi Berra— observed a lot by watching. What I've observed is that there are lots of reasons why we have invented so many religions. They provide solace and comfort in a world that furnishes nothing but ambiguity, loose ends, unanswered questions and dangling …

(Those are all the same thing, aren't they? Hmmm. "Take two" [clap!].)

… solace and comfort in a world that furnishes nothing but ambiguity, injustice, pain, plague, devastation, death, dry skin and cellulite.

---

19 Campaign slogans notwithstanding.

It's all too much to bear, so people create coping mechanisms such as religion, fermentation, and ...

Well, religion and fermentation. A discussion of fermentation is beyond the scope of this scholarly work, so we shall stick to the much simpler subject of Religion.

All religions are efforts to answer one timeless, cosmic question:

Why does my life suck?

There are two basic answers to this question:

1) We evolved accidentally from Paramecia and along the way developed sufficient intellectual capacity to:

- Notice that our life sucks, and,

- Wonder why.

2) A Supreme Being with either a sick sense of humor or a serious malevolent streak created us and put us here to Suffer. In Gratitude for the opportunity to Suffer, we must Worship Him. Whenever we find ourselves wondering Why He Would Treat Us Like Shit, we must gather with other Believers and sing, recite texts, clasp hands and do other stuff to distract ourselves from noticing that the original question remains unanswered. This process shall be known as Fellowship.

Most folks are so uncomfortable with the first, most-likely answer that they cling desperately to some version of the second, so-implausible-as-to-be-laughable-if-it-weren't-so-universally-held, one.

Liberals, however, must cope with an additional level of discomfort: religion itself.[20] This is caused by several features inherent to religion, including:

- Its fundamental incompatibility with science;

- Its basis in Faith rather than Reason;

- Its foundation in conservative values;

---

20 Unless it is an election cycle. Then they all profess to believe in God.

- Its typical subordination of women;
- Its relationship to the Republican Party, and, I suspect most important;
- Its prohibition of all sorts of stuff like premarital sex, blow jobs, homosexuality, abortion, drugs, lust, greed, gambling, drunkenness, orgies, Vietnamese bud, beer bongs, personal vibrators, party-harnesses, Swedish films[21] and the use of vegetable oil for activities other than cooking.

Obviously, if you want to Rock N' Roll, religion has got to go.

So, if it happens that you are in a group that really, really wants to engage in taboo behavior such as the stuff on the previous list (or you happen to buy into that whole Darwin thing) then you must drop out of the Church and become a Secular Humanist.

But whether you are a Tome-Thumping Fundamentalist Believer or a Rational Liberal Scientist, the Big Question remains unanswered, so you find that you still need to gather with like-minded souls for solace, fellowship and comfort— temporary relief from the unending assault of ambiguity that is life on Planet Earth.

I think liberal people have morphed their political cause into a Neo-Religion because (gasp!) there is something religion provides that they can't get as Atheists, Agnostics, Secular Humanists, Universalists, Congregationalists or the other watered-down versions of religion available to them within the Liberal milieu. Something still seems to be missing: solidarity; fellowship; shared beliefs. Good pie. Sing-alongs.

Because the itch for solace can't be relieved with the Secular Humanist salve, they've done what people have always done: strip out the irritating parts of the too-restrictive belief system and make a new one with more loopholes. That is how we get religions like Congregationalism, where a parish can be run by a bitter, Marxist lesbian minister who studiously avoids mentioning God during services so as not to offend the tithing Atheists who are sitting in the pews.

---

21 I don't care *what* your moral or political leanings are— Swedish films should be banned, period.

My "birth-church," the Episcopal, was created in just such a manner. One of the English Kings Henry wanted to pork/marry his girlfriend but the buzz-kill Pope wouldn't give him a divorce. Bummer.

> "Well, prithee," (or something like that) says the King, "I'm the frigging King, am I not?"

So he started his own church and told the Pope to take a hike. All the Catholics moved to Ireland, the Church of England was born, and there's been nothing but bloodshed since. But, the King got his divorce and his girl (who was "face-caught-fire-and-her-Mum-beat-it-out-with-a-rake" ugly, if you ask me).[22]

So, my church descended from that one, and it's basically Catholicism minus a few irritations (Latin, confession, Guilt), plus a few upgrades and enhancements (divorce and …   OK, just divorce.). Well, actually, that's not entirely accurate. Episcopal clergy can marry, so they tend not to rape the altar boys. As much.

Nevertheless, I submit that Progressive Liberalism has evolved (and I don't use that term without a keen appreciation of the irony involved) to provide a more user-friendly replacement for traditional religion— one that delivers the solidarity/fellowship/certainty benefits while requiring fewer behavioral and/or moral restrictions so everyone can still have a good time and the President can screw around on his wife— which any French or Italian President has been able do for quite some time without anyone saying a damned word about it, I might add.

Progressive Liberalism deserves kudos for its handsome record of resistance to the inevitable collapse into a belief system. Sadly, as of the 2008 election, and the emergence of the Obama Children's Chorus, the transformation into a fully functioning religion is complete.

---

22 Granted, this is but an historically approximate account. I got the big chunks mostly right: the divorce, the porking and the ugly chick.

Well now that everyone is pissed off, we may as well move on. Next, we'll explore the yawning chasms of the human cognitive "system." I promise to cover this subject with the same intellectual rigor that you have come to expect from your reading so far.

Part Three:

COGNITIVE TRAPS

This would be fun if it weren't so frightening. We're about to plumb the cognitive processes that allow extremists to contemplate and adopt various concepts that form the foundations of their beliefs, and to firmly clutch those beliefs without noticing that they are often based on fundamentally flawed drivel.

These mental mechanisms make it possible to believe, for example, that an omniscient/omnipotent God, when desiring to communicate with the lowly beings that He has created, would do so by sending the message via a talking salamander, channeling through someone who suffers from migraine auras, or by creating a bunch of bananas that— when viewed from a certain angle— resembles a portrait of his Only Begotten Son.[1]

Here's a guy who can communicate with us any way he wants to, such as sending an e-mail to every address on earth at the same time, skywriting with no airplane, or incinerating the whole planet, but instead he chooses, *every time*, to talk to us in the most ambiguous way possible. His followers, rather than conclude that he's actually not there at all, make up explanations: "He works in mysterious ways."

Religious extremists aren't the only ones who do this. Lefties came up with Political Correctness, after all— a denial of reality at least as egregious as any religious belief.

This discussion will help us understand how people can get their thoughts so twisted up that they could justify burning a ski resort to the ground— in the middle of a forest— in the name of environmentalism.

Ready for some rollicking good fun?

---

1 Who no living person has ever seen, of course.

ONE THING'S FOR SURE:
NOTHING.

Ambiguity. I'm not sure how I really feel about it. On one hand, I kinda' like it— it's good for creativity. It helps me think of new ideas and unique solutions to problems. On the other hand, it can be quite uncomfortable, even physically so, sometimes causing considerable stress. On another hand, some of my best ideas come from ambiguous situations. On yet another hand, I'm not sure I'd miss it if it disappeared altogether. But then again, how boring would it be if everything was known? That sounds like a pretty rigid and cold existence. Ambiguity or clarity? Clarity or ambiguity? Gee, I just don't know ...

People HATE ambiguity. We want answers and we want them *now*. It is like a nagging headache, or chronic tinnitus, or a dripping faucet.[2] Ambiguity is the ultimate cognitive pain for many people, and they will do anything to make it stop, including the techniques outlined below.

BRIDGE FOR SALE. INQUIRE WITHIN (YOURSELF).

Human beings are arguably one of the more intelligent species,[3] but, unfortunately, along with that intelligence comes a propensity to be hornswoggled. We have an impressive capacity to amass information coupled with a stinking-lousy ability to determine the veracity of that information— assuming we even care.

This hornswoggling comes from many sources, such as con artists, politicians, salespeople, lovers, family members, teachers, advertisers, religious leaders and others who want us to do, think and believe things that are in the interests of the swoggler and not necessarily the swogglee.

But the most frequent and most dangerous hornswoggling comes from our own flawed cognitive systems. We have the unique (as far as

---

2 Or a ticking clock, or a dog barking all night, or living near an airport, or Ravel's Bolero, or the incessant hum of fluorescent lights, or ...

3 I'm not personally advancing that argument, mind you, but many others have. Name one other species that has developed the capability of being totally full of shit.

anyone can tell) ability to observe reality and reach utterly, profoundly, often dangerously incorrect conclusions about what we see, almost every time. And to do this, somehow, without being eliminated from the gene pool.

This is why some people, for example, will unfailingly believe in conspiracy theories regardless of the paucity of real evidence to support the theory. (Hey— you with the plastic Spock ears! Nothing significant happened at Area 51. Let it go.)

Others will repeat the same behavior all their lives without ever noticing that it doesn't achieve the desired results. War protesters and religious proselytizers are two examples that come swiftly to mind.

Jesse Jackson[4] called it "Stinkin' Thinkin'." Dr. Phil says, "How's that workin' for you?" They're referring to the same thing: cognitive traps— the sneaky little tricks our brains play on us, that make us believe all sorts of nonsense, such as:

- He's going to leave her and marry me.
- Someone should give a shit what I think down here in the mail room.
- I'm the best sexual partner he/she's ever had.
- Jesus will appear as a stain on a potato sack.
- He's really sorry this time and will stop hitting me.
- These pants make my butt look good.
- All we need to do is increase awareness and things will change.
- My candidate is really going to do what he promised during the campaign.

The lion's share of our self-inflicted hornswoggling is the result of a small but important group of cognitive errors. These are:

1. Seeing patterns in information that are not there.
2. Failing to see patterns that are.

---

4 At least I think it was he.

3. Inventing simple answers to complex questions.

4. Inventing complex answers to simple questions.

Other reasoning defects that we will explore include confirmation bias, zero-sum thinking, ambiguity intolerance, circular reasoning, cognitive dissonance and myriad other mind-games that get us into trouble inside our own heads. It seems almost as if we are designed to misinterpret as a default condition, causing one to wonder how we survived the evolutionary process at all.[5]

Activists utilize imaginative combinations of these cognitive defects to get behind completely unfounded theories and/or beliefs, amass copious quantities of misinformation to support those beliefs, then form action plans based on unrealistic and unachievable goals that, invariably, involve lobbying, proselytizing, haranguing, lecturing or otherwise bugging people like me.

A number of possibilities might explain why we possess these cognitive peculiarities:

- They are vestiges of some poorly understood evolutionary advantages that aided our survival for eons, but are no longer useful in modern civilization;

- God has a very dark sense of humor;

- We are too smart for our own good;

- We are not nearly as self-aware as we would prefer to think;

- We are not, in fact, the most-evolved species on Earth.[6]

Cognitive traps help extremists believe truly baffling ideas that are essential to making their belief systems operate. Herewith, a review of some of the most-popular cognitive traps employed by partisans:

---

5 Religious people, of course, don't believe we did. They believe we were formed just as we are— fully fucked up— in one shot. Perhaps we are, in fact, a crude prototype. That might explain a lot.

6 For that I would nominate cats, who never work and can make slaves out of humans.

BLACK AND WHITE
(non-racial discussion)

A Black/White mentality is one of the staples of extremist pathology (along with other variants such as Win/Lose: see below). This way of seeing things conveys one important benefit to the user: cognitive economy. With this method, one doesn't need to waste a lot of time parsing nuance, digging around in detail, or peering into murky gray areas. These forms of responsible analytical exercise are time-consuming, vexing pursuits that often lead right back to the most-dreaded of all mental states for the extremist:

Ambiguity.

Ambiguity is the default condition of reality.[7] This idea frightens the extremist more than anything else, because it blows down the neat, cozy dogma house that he is curled up inside. Extremist viewpoints are threatened by ambiguity because it is the solvent that melts the glue of their belief system— which, ironically, is designed to banish ambiguity in the first place.

The black/white philosophy makes it easier to navigate the vast sea of nuance in which we are all adrift, by making it possible to quickly identify certain important information, without the bothersome task of actually learning about the subject. Among the "fast facts" that one can obtain using black/white thinking are:

- Who is an Idiot;
- Who is a Sinner;
- Which 99.99% of all information should be dismissed out-of-hand;
- Which .01% of all information should be embraced, inflated, distorted and endlessly repeated.

The huge cognitive savings that can be realized with this method can thus be applied to lecturing, haranguing, proselytizing, resigned

---

7 As far as I can tell.

sighing, eye-rolling, Bible-thumping, Marching on Washington and other activities useful in the harassment of the rest of us.

Here's how black-and-white thinking works with the two groups featured in this book:

Ultraconservatives:

"Things Are the way they Are. I am basically happy, or if not, at least numbed by Faith, therefore my happiness must be linked to the way Things Are. Change is a threat to my happiness. Change is bad."

Ultraliberals:

"Things Are the way they Are. I am basically unhappy, or if not, unhappy on behalf of some victim group, therefore my unhappiness must be linked to the way Things Are. Change is the road to happiness. Change is good.

Both groups pay a high price for their respective mind sets;

Group one ignores the possibilities of changes that might make them better off because they are afraid to take the risk that things might get worse (Keep baby. Keep bath water. Add to previously retained bath water [yecch].).

Group two will eliminate the things that are good because they can't identify the aspects of their unhappiness that are unrelated to the environment they inhabit (Drown baby. Throw out bath water and baby carcass. Throw out crib. Burn house. Move to Portland.).

Neither group, however, pays as high a price as the Middle, who must contend with both of them, constantly. The middle is obliged to defend that which is good against rabid change agents, and to contend with the reluctance of the other group to embrace change of any kind, however beneficial.

People who live in a black-and-white world are lucky in one respect. They only have to be unhappy with 50% of everything, a 50% that is very easy to identify. And of course, unhappy is precisely what they are— so they never stop complaining. The other extremists are unhappy with the other 50% of everything, and they never stop complaining either.

For the Middle, someone is complaining about 100% of everything, all the time.

ALL AND NOTHING.

Win/lose reasoning is a malignant variant of black/white that has spread throughout every layer of American society— primarily through ESPN, which provides something like five thousand channels of programming material dedicated solely to the theme of winning and losing. The allocation of two thirds of our society's communications bandwidth to competitive-event programming has led Americans to believe that all forms of social interaction are win/lose challenges. This includes matrimony, career building, ordering from a restaurant menu, lawn care, merging to a single lane, school enrollment, fashion and makeup choices, financial compensation, thinness, hair growth, child-rearing, material acquisition, tanning, all forms of discussion on any subject, and every level of election politics, from the U.S. Presidential election all the way down to the most local, venal and pernicious of all forms of government: the Condominium Association.

We compete to show who knows more about organic farming by paying seven dollars for a carrot at Whole Foods®. We build huge, Jumbotron-enhanced churches to prove our sanctimony. We hire snarling lawyers to fuck over our obsolete spouses at the expense of our children's sanity. We drive fuel-slurping Hummers[8] just to show who is a Player and who is a Loser.

Americans are obsessed with scoreboards, and none more than activists. In the American political system, all sorts of corny concepts such as stewardship of our collective resources, sacrifice for the common good, creation of a Rising Tide for All Boats, and "We're all in

---

8 Since this writing, it seems Hummers are going extinct. It will be interesting to see how those people will convey their disdain for the environment in the future. Rape Bambi?

this together" must take a back seat to the primary activity: crushing your opponents face-first into the mire with the jack-boots of righteous rage.

I'm not saying that doesn't sound like lots of fun, mind you.

Anyway, from the vantage point of the Middle, it appears that our society's two main antagonists have long forgotten what they were originally fighting about, and are now just trying to annihilate one another. Our lives, our society and our country are caught in the crossfire of this perpetual Hatfield/McCoy feud between the Extreme Right and the Extreme Left. It's not about issues any longer. It's just about winning.

As a fellow Middle, you may be interested in how this Win/Lose system works. Here are the operational rules of Win/Lose thinking, as practiced by our political adversaries:

- If you won, I must have lost.
- If you lost, I must have won, however,
- If you lost but you're not unhappy, I didn't really win.
- If I can rub your face in the shit, I don't care if I win or not.
- If I have to lose to insure that you lose, too, I'm willing to do so, however,
- If I won, but so did you, that ruins it for me, so I lost.
- I will pretend to endorse a win/win situation if the game is rigged in my favor.
- If you won, you must have cheated. I'll take this all the way to the Supreme Court.
- If you won without cheating, I'll still take it all the way to the Supreme Court.
- If the Supreme Court decides in your favor, I'll pack the Court with people who agree with me and wait as long as it takes to win, regardless of the unintended consequences.

- If the Supreme Court decides in my favor, I will oppose every nomination you make, regardless of the damage to the nominee, the Court, the country or any combination thereof.
- I will never accept any outcome I don't like.

ZERO-SUM THINKING

Zero-sum thinking is closely related to Win/Lose. In fact, it is so similar that it's possible that this and the previous section are describing the same thing, adding nothing to this book other than increased length. I don't care. I prefer to think of this section as yet another beautifully crafted, concise and witty nugget of social commentary equal to the preceding ones, so I'm including it anyway.

The basic tenet of Zero-Sum Thinking is this: There's only so much of a thing to go around (money, love, sex, food, happiness, power), so every *iota* that you have of a desired thing comes out of my share of that same thing. This is why we hate rich people: they screwed us out of our rightful share of the proverbial pie. Never mind that they might have had a great idea and did what it takes to bring it successfully to market, worked their asses off, put up significant capital, risked failure and bankruptcy, employed a bunch of people or in some other way created wealth— [9] and that we, by contrast, are a bunch of lazy whiners. They have cool stuff and we don't— we got screwed!

If you see the world this way, you are doomed to spend the rest of your life fighting.

COGNITIVE DISSONANCE:
THE PERPETUAL INNER ARGUMENT

When I wrote this snippet, I was *not* watching the "historic" debate between Senator Joe Biden and Governor Sarah Palin. I didn't have any idea whether Joe was chewing up and spitting out the Governette

---

9 This is a concept that many people will deny is even possible. In their mind set, anything that you acquire comes out of someone's hide.

or spinning a touching yarn about Abe Lincoln's first radio broadcast. I was sure I'd hear all about it the next morning.

One thing that struck me about these two candidates was the deep irony of their respective selections as running mates. Before Biden came on board, the Obama campaign was hammering McCain about his age and his long entrenchment in "the system." He was being described as an ancient Washington insider— while Obama, by contrast, was a fresh, new "outsider." So what did Obama do? He selected the next-most-entrenched wheezing Washington insider as a running mate, because he added "maturity" to the ticket.

Meanwhile, McCain was blasting Obama about "inexperience": "he's not seasoned enough to lead." So he picks Sarah Palin, to add "youth" to the ticket.

In order for the two parties and their supporters to remain blind to the irony of the situation, they had to employ a technique known as Cognitive Dissonance: the ability to hold two contradictory ideas in one's head at the same time. Cognitive dissonance is necessary for extremists to function because they all ascribe to belief systems that are impossible to adhere to faithfully. A few examples:

The religious/morality extremists must cope with the idea that they are supposed to repress all sorts of corporeal urges because they are sins against God, while accepting the fact that God gave them the urges in the first place.[10] In order to hold these two concepts simultaneously, you need to use cognitive dissonance. This also goes for the question: "Why does God let innocent little babies die?"

Extreme Liberals need it too. One can blather all one wants to when it's philosophical, but very few of us are truly color-blind when there's an offspring and an engagement ring involved. But let's suppose that you *really are* cool with Sydney Poitier coming to dinner. What if your carefully groomed liberal-arts daughter brings home a Skinhead with a swastika tattooed on his scalp? In order to be truly "Liberal" and allow Meighan to "make her own choices," you're going to need— yep, cognitive dissonance. It's the only way out of the dilemma.

---

10 I know— He's "testing" us. Constantly. What kind of prick would do that to another being?

Here is a short list of things that are enabled by cognitive dissonance:

- Supporting human rights and being a Marxist
- Killing abortion doctors
- Protecting free speech and supporting political correctness
- Protesting banking corruption while demanding to be released from your student loan obligation
- Urging tolerance of Muslim culture and being a feminist
- Being a fundamentalist preacher and a homosexual
- Buggering a 12-year-old and calling it "horsing around"

Belief systems are by nature very rigid, and therefore brittle.[11] They rely heavily on cognitive dissonance to cope with contradictory evidence, and more important, to allow the believers to violate the tenets of the system while continuing to believe they are true believers.

I KNEW I WAS RIGHT— EVERYTHING PROVES IT.

Have you ever noticed that a red light turns green at the *exact* moment your car comes to a complete stop?

It doesn't. No more often than at any other moment in the stopping process, such as when you're three-quarters "stopped," just-starting-to-stop, considering stopping or breezing through the intersection. We don't think of "stopping" as a process, but only as an end result: stopped. That's why we only make note of the coincidence when the light turns green at the exact moment when the car rocks back and delivers that little 'whip' on your neckbones. It's a syndrome known as Confirmation Bias, and it manifests itself as the tendency to notice information that confirms your beliefs while ignoring information that is contradictory. It happens subconsciously as a defense mechanism against the discomfort of ambiguity.

---

11 Theodore Dalrymple's term.

Confirmation bias makes it possible to notice all sorts of information that reinforces your beliefs and preconceptions, while ignoring contradictory data, no matter how much there is. Extremists employ this to great effect by saturating themselves with confirmatory information while studiously avoiding sources that might supply contradictory material. At no time does confirmation bias become more pernicious than during gatherings of believers, when folks get together to celebrate how enlightened/pissed off they are.

Confirmation bias creates such powerful cognitive urges in people that they begin to ignore the poor quality of the information being considered and of the sources providing it, resulting in the growing tendency to believe anything they hear either for or against their pet subject. Eventually, they believe anything, no matter how farfetched, regardless of the blowhard that's delivering it. Think Hannity. Or Huffington.

Taken to the extreme, confirmation bias allows the True Believer to include the *lack* of information as confirmatory data to support his beliefs, as in:

> "The government refuses to tell us what is inside Area 51, which proves there is a conspiracy to hide something from us."

This proves nothing of the sort, of course. Perhaps the only thing it proves is that the Army no longer has a budget for holding press conferences to deny that something happened sixty years ago.

COINCIDENCE, CORRELATION, CAUSATION:
Confusion, Chaos, Calamity

Some people say that there is no such thing as a coincidence. It is no coincidence that these people believe in all kinds of appallingly stupid shit. If one of your cognitive imperatives is that everything must have Meaning, then you are going to need to exert tremendous energy making up explanations for things that may not actually have one. The bus driver didn't see your grandmother, okay? That's it.

Humans have a frightening inability to discern the differences among coincidence, correlation and causation. Maybe it's because they all start with the same letter and have too many syllables ("C-hummena-hummena" vs: "C-hummena-hummena"). This deficiency causes untold damage to human progress by allowing us to incorrectly conclude that all sorts of things have meaningful relationships that don't, in fact, exist. Then we act on this "information."[12]

Eons ago, some Neanderthal noticed that a volcano erupted on the same day his wife died. Putting two and two together (figuratively— we hadn't invented mathematics yet), he deduced that there was an Angry God in the volcano, and so he (*coincidentally* being the Chief) subsequently decreed that the firstborn daughter of each couple (where this *correlation* came from is anyone's guess) should henceforth be thrown into the volcano, for the purpose of preventing unnecessary deaths caused by cranky Deities. Fourteen million babies were incinerated before a new religion replaced this misguided belief system.

Then along come the Cro-Magnons™, a more-developed new version of the hominid product line (All New, "Hi-Slope" Foreheads! 30% Less "Hunch"! No Knuckle-Dragging!). They took one look at that "Volcano God" silliness ("What would you expect, Doris? They're Neanderthals.") and started their own religion— one without the "obvious" flaws of the previous one.

This new religion was based on the now-obvious "fact" that the Fertility God was transported across the sky in the pouch of a winged marmot, and that if the Spirits were having a Cosmic-Deity Hoedown inside their subterranean Secret Kingdom only accessible through a portal in the lost underwater city of Blubblub, AND you had exercised the foresight to prepare a potion of chicken blood, goat excrement and bees knees (with just a hint of coriander), slathering the resulting mixture on your ding-dong, your crops would be plentiful.

Further, the practice of hurling infants into boiling caldera was considered to be appallingly primitive behavior by this new group—

---

12 Why? Because "someone needs to 'do something.'" Extremists are completely uncomfortable with the idea that there are situations where you simply can't "do" anything.

any idiot could see that you should cut their little hearts out with a blade of sharpened obsidian.

This theology, however, was replaced by yet another, which was replaced by yet another, and so on for millennia, with the predictable result of the appalling slaughter of untold numbers of innocents (all in the name of "protecting us").

Folk remedies are another example: "I drank some twiddle-root tea and I didn't catch a cold." There is no way to convince this person that he or she might not have caught the cold anyway, or that a cold was even imminent. The tea prevented it— that's all there is to it.

Below are a few possible explanations for this person's experience:

- Twiddle-root tea prevents the common cold.
- She was getting a cold, and her body's defenses fought it off.
- She has allergies, and mistook them for the onset of a cold.
- The cold was imaginary.

The only thing that you can say for certain in all of these examples is that a bunch of stuff happened at the same time. That's it. Sorry.

In the interest of Human Progress[13], let's try to get a better grasp on the three Cs: Coincidence, Correlation, and Causation:

COINCIDENCE— This is a condition when one or more things occur simultaneously or in a *perceived* sequence. For example: you're in a bar, looking good. You approach an attractive young lady, put on a little swagger, and deliver your best line. The next morning you wake up and have an awkward breakfast before promising to get together again.

What happened? You might be tempted to conclude that something about your appearance, demeanor, wit, charm, pecs, buns, or other attributes caused the little honey to decide to go to your place for some torrid knee-knockin'. You would infer a *causal* relationship between your performance and the outcome. This would be incorrect. You got your wick dipped because of the *coincidence* of being the first

---

13 Right— follow *me* to the Promised Land. That should turn out well.

non-repulsive guy with a full set of limbs and two eyeballs who showed up after *she* decided she wanted to get some chub.

The ramifications of this misconception can be expensive and destructive. Here are just a few of the possible consequences of seeing a false causal relationship in this situation:

- You will probably use that same line again.
- You will buy more clothes from that store.
- You may take dance lessons.
- You will go to the same bar for the next several years and never get lucky again, while wasting enough time and money to get a Master's degree.
- You will have that same haircut for the rest of your life.

CORRELATION— This is a condition where two or more things (events, facts, etc.) have *some kind* of relationship. The exact nature and direction of the relationship is not always obvious, and can be obscured by having a number of variables that might— or might not— be pertinent.

Let's re-run the scenario above, while changing only one parameter (this is what us Scientists call an Experimental Control):

Everything in the scenario is identical, except after delivery of your brilliant line, she tells you to "pound sand" and spins around on her bar stool, leaving you to feel like a total lame-ass.

This is where things can get confusing. It is possible that the only reason you got rejected was because she just wasn't in the mood— and that otherwise you would have soon been steering your Pleasure Boat down her River of Ecstasy. In this case, the soul-crushing blow to your person would still be a coincidence. But …

… and here's where it gets even more murky: she might have rejected you for any one, combination of some of, or all of, the traits you displayed in that fabulous come-on. But which ones?

At this point you have a dilemma: There *may* be a *correlation* between one or more of your traits and your rejection, or maybe not. You have no data. Is it your hair? Your breath? What?

This is the juncture where most people are so uncomfortable with the uncertainty of the situation that they invent some meaning and act on it. Total makeover. Join a fitness club. Learn to cook. Turn gay. Study bomb making— whatever. However, the smartest and most-economical (but counterintuitive) response to the situation is to realize that you have insufficient data to even form an hypothesis, much less conclude anything, and to wait until you can gather more experimental data. This is uncomfortable for most people, so they grab whatever meaning they can find, no matter the cost.

CAUSATION— This is a condition where one thing causes another thing to happen. This is the most-direct relationship in the triad. Again, we shall re-run the experiment while changing one parameter:

Everything in the scenario is identical except you wake up the next morning in your apartment, lying in a pool of your own blood. Your wallet and every valuable in the place is gone, your identity has been sold to Indonesian gangsters, your penis is three blocks away in a vacant lot, and there is a blog about you— complete with photos and grainy video of you dancing in ladies' underwear— which has already received 4.2 million page-views.

This is a *causal* relationship, pig.

THE SEARCH FOR MEANING

You've just learned that your grandmother was hit by a bus. Splattered over a half-block of shops, offices, hot-dog carts and newsstands. Tufts of blue hair cling to a barely-dented bumper on the Evening News.

After you experience the Five Stages of Grief (Shock, Denial, Litigation, Settlement, Acceptance), the next thing that enters your mind is:

Why?

Why did this happen to such a lovely woman? Such a giving and caring person, who cooked the meals, cleaned the house, wiped the noses and patiently sat in that old rocker darning socks while Grandpa was down in the basement playing with each of the kids until they reached puberty.

Why did this happen? Why, *why*, WHY?…

OK, take a deep breath, and don't worry. An explanation is at hand. All you need to do is pick one that makes you feel better. And there are plenty of reasons that people will come up with to help you cope. Some examples:

- Jesus took Gram to be in Heaven with all the babies that died before they could be baptized (Note to Jesus: Wouldn't a light tap on the shoulder have worked just as well as a bus impact? Especially for such a generous woman? Just asking).
- The bus driver was under-trained because the Republican budget cuts eliminated a vital safety program.
- If the bus hadn't been full of illegal Wetbacks it wouldn't have been there in the first place.
- I don't know what happened, but I'm sure the World Bank was involved somehow.
- Did you see the "grassy knoll" in the background? Did you?

Any of these explanations might be correct, but there's another one that has special resonance for me— one that explains the whole event with crystalline clarity:

- Granny was in the middle of the street at the wrong time.

Naaah. That can't be it. Can we see the list again?

When shit happens, we humans just *have* to find an explanation— something that reveals the meaning of the horrible event— and if we can't find one, we go completely nuts.

No other creature on the planet spends its time searching for meaning.

Snails don't do it:

"Hey, whatever happened to Bob?"

"Beats me. I heard someone speaking French, and the next thing I knew, he was gone. Say, is there any good lichen over there? This rock is tapped out."

Dolphins don't do it:

"Aren't you sick of playing with this stupid ball all day?"

"Of course I am, Bob. But it's what we do. The killer whale splashes the crowd; the seals wallow around and make fart noises; and the dolphins play with the ball. That's just the natural order of thi— Hey, look! It's a BALL! Woohoo!"

Not even Bonobos, the celebrated Nurturing Feminist Monkeys, do it.

"Bob's dead!"

"Who gives a shit? He was just a male, and he's already impregnated Doris, Mabel, and Sutubanawabananna, so he's useless around here. Besides, he'd just be a drain on our precious natural resources— drinking all the fermented spit and organizing stupid sports-betting leagues. Now, run along and point out your brother's inherent deficiencies."

No, only Humans have the ability to Search For Meaning. And the one thing you can count on is this: once the search starts, they are DAMNED WELL GOING TO FIND SOME MEANING. Flaubert[14] termed this phenomenon the "Rage to Conclude."

---

14 Gratuitous, cloying reference to a famous novelist— preferably French.

Why do we do this? Because we can.[15]

It's possible that we are all on this earthly plane because of some random accident: a swarthy carbon atom sidles up to a hot little minx of a hydrogen atom in some volcanic hot tub and schwing!, life erupts.

I can't help wondering (see how we are?) whether our ability to find meaning didn't come about in a similar way. Neuron A snuggles up to Synapse B inside some protohuman's brain. Wants to "cuddle."

"Hey, Darlin'. Nice dendrites!"

"Get bent, pig. You're Reason, I'm Emotion. We're not supposed to commingle."

"But, Darlin', remember the last time you told me to 'get bent', and the time before that— and the time before that?"

"Sure. I also told you not to call me 'Darlin'. Not only are you dense, but you don't listen, either. What's new about that?"

"Don't you see a pattern developin' here? Don't that mean anything to you?"

"Yeah, it means you're developing a pattern of being annoying. So what? Now, get bent."

"Aw, c'mon baby, you gotta' admit there's something special goin' on here. There's a reason why we're always fussin' and fightin' like this. C'mon, just let me just spoon with ya' fer a little while…"

"Well, you are kinda cute…"

---

15 There's a riddle about dogs …

Just like that— by accident— we change from a species that's perfectly happy to eat, procreate, poop in the woods and run around naked, to one that's festooned with warlike religions, conspiracy theories, political parties, self-help groups, bloggers, televangelists, New Age retreats, funeral directors, palm readers, and talk radio.

Ever since we developed the ability to derive meaning, we've never looked back. And we find it everywhere: rust spots on the old refrigerator, cloud patterns, the position of the planets[16], and practically anything that anyone decides is "showing a pattern."

We just can't accept the idea that we might be floating in a Sea of Randomness, with stinging, "Shit-happens" Jellyfish all around us and "His-number-just-came-up" Sharks cruising below. We all want The Lifeguard of Explanation to…

(nah. That metaphor won't stretch any farther without snapping. My apologies.)

Where were we?

Meaning. The principal trouble with meaning is that it is always speculative, subject to doubt, vulnerable to new information, and thus volatile. We need it desperately, but we can't hold on to it, and every new piece of information has the power to shatter it into splinters, rendering our whole world view pointless and void.

Other than that, have a nice day.

LONG ODDS

Dirk brushed the perfectly placed curl back from his rugged-yet-appropriately moisturized (he was a modern man, after all) forehead. Now that everyone had seen how masculinely disheveled it made him appear, he was going to need his eyes for pursuits other than breaking hearts.

The mountain— K2— had been conquered many times, but not like

---

16 Just curious— what if the maternity nurse had broken into the drug locker the morning you were born, and was so baked on Valium at your delivery that she wrote the wrong date and time on your birth certificate? Do you end up with someone else's horoscope?

this. Not only was Dirk planning to scale the massif without oxygen, he was planning a romantic encounter at the summit with none other than the delicious starlet Jessica Simpson. He shouldered his immense pack, which contained all the accoutrements for the soiree: a nice, but not-too-ostentatious Brut, elegant collapsible stemware for two, a selection of fromages from the best regions of Normandie, a solar-powered Bose Wave®, his beloved iPod® touch, the classic red-checkered tablecloth, a small butane warming oven, and of course, Ms. Simpson herself, thoroughly insulated from the numbing cold, despite wearing her Daisy Duke outfit.

Dirk acknowledged that he was taking on a daunting challenge, but as he told the assembled reporters: "If it's worth doing… It's worth overdoing."

"That's why I'm going up there in my boxers."

Some people are attracted to lost causes, uphill battles and hopeless efforts, possibly because long odds make them believe that the payoff will be higher if, somehow, they can prevail. This is the only explanation I can conjure for someone to, for example, form an organization to try to get teenagers to stop screwing.

Seriously, you might as well oppose, say, weather.

Not just certain kinds of weather, but the whole idea.

That sure doesn't stop extremists, though, and when it comes to odds— the longer the better. There's something compelling about achieving the impossible that attracts certain people to a Cause.

There also seems to be an approximate correlation between the length of the activist's chosen odds, and his need to recruit *me* to do some mule work. Obviously, if someone's dream is some Cheops-level accomplishment, they are going to need a lot of slaves who don't mind being crushed to death during construction. This is where you and I come in. Meanwhile, the activist— like Cheops— cannot get his hands dirty because he's doing the "visionary" work.

Despite the fact that the long odds are what make the Cause so compelling, the activist is, paradoxically, so completely oblivious to implausibility that he cannot be convinced that his dream is bullshit. The more skepticism he encounters, the harder he works at revealing the Truth, spreading the Word, and trying to harness you and me to the traces of his theology.

until…

THE TERRIFYING POWER OF CERTAINTY

There exists no person more frightening to a Middle than someone who possesses Certainty. It is impossible to overestimate the destruction caused by people who have adopted beliefs that provide this attribute. Through the use of the various cognitive tools described earlier (and others not discussed here), True Believers can reach a state of warm, satisfying self-delusion known as Certainty.

Under this banner, people have justified the most heinous of crimes against humanity, other species, the environment, freedom of thought, expression and religion, and human dignity, just to name a few.

It would be easy to reel off the crimes of religious zealotry, such as the Crusades, the Inquisition, 9/11, Jonestown and other low-hanging fruit, leaving the Left without any indictments. But the left has its own crimes to account for, such as its abysmal failure to reform American education— despite countless attempts— and the wake of self-absorbed dumbshits left behind. Then there's Lyndon Johnson's *War to Increase and Prolong Poverty So White People Can Feel Good About Themselves for Caring*. And don't forget the incomprehensible deification of scores of Marxist murderers— like the 26-year-old rich kid from Argentina who, through his sophomoric idealism, helped enslave untold numbers of innocents in squalor and misery. Plus, I can't stand that beret.[17]

People who have the wisdom to know their own ignorance don't start bloody crusades, malignant political movements, dictatorial cults, "whatever-isms" or other institutions to boss everyone else around. But without the humility that comes with accurate self-knowledge, people get all sorts of crazy ideas about their own infallibility.

---

17 As you have already learned.

That brand of Certainty has brought us many, if not most, of the world's ills. Idealists are the scariest when they decide they are going to "save" or "liberate" the rest of us from some perceived evil. When they get that look in their eyes, we Middles need to dive for cover because it is our blood— figuratively, at minimum— that is going to be spilled in the name of a Great Cause.

Part Four:

OPERATIONAL METHODOLOGIES

I thought that was fun, didn't you? Onward, then, brave Middle!

In this section, we will examine how extremists go about the business of interfering with everyone else's business. Included in this part are group-dynamic methods that they use to stay excited about the issues, recruit fresh idealists, and distort information to their tastes. Later, we'll explore tools and tactics that are employed to foist the results on everyone else. You'll love it— let's get started!

PEER REVUE: LET'S HAVE COFFEE
AND AGREE WITH EACH OTHER!

Cloistering and Festering (CloisterFest! XVII) is an important ritual used to maintain solidarity and fellowship among extremists. In this ritual, the True Believers gather in a chapel, cave, coffee shop (an indie, of course— never Starbucks), campsite, compound,[1] Hollywood mansion, or other suitable venue. Then, after carefully screening the guest list for dissenters, the Believers dine on delicious hors' d' oeuvres, spit-roasted goat and virgin boys, consecrated wafers, absinthe, breakfast pancakes, granola bars or other appropriate fare, and repeat their mantras to one another until they are all whipped into a froth of self-righteous smugness and justified rage against their enemies. —Hey! It's also a fund-raiser, so bring your checkbook!

One result of this CloisterFest process is that the participants eventually develop a world view that is both passionately held and fatally inaccurate. This is because of another human cognitive defect: the inability to distinguish between an unchallenged assertion and a fact.[2]

When people of like minds gather for a CloisterFest, they encounter lots of head-nodding, clucking and other forms of assent that leave them with the false impression that "everyone" agrees with them. The more CloisterFesting that takes place, the more "everyone" is in agree-

---

1 This can be on Martha's Vineyard or deep in the South Dakota wilderness. The important feature is the high wall, razor-wire fence, or other barrier to keep out contradictory ideas.

2 Closely related, research shows, to the inability to distinguish between one's ass and a hole in the ground— a more widely recognized condition.

ment. If people are immersed in enough of this mutual affirmation, they can get the impression that their views are concurrent with reality, no matter how farfetched they actually are.

Of course, that's the purpose of the CloisterFest: to get together for cross-parroting, circular reasoning, perusal of patently nonobjective periodicals, books, films and documentaries, and the general stoking of the fires of outrage/fear/paranoia/smugness/bliss/rapture/whatever. CloisterFesters go to a great deal of trouble to avoid information that challenges their world view because it provides comfort by supplying answers to life's nagging questions. So what if the answers aren't true? They feel good and make life tolerable, whether you're frightened by human sexuality, horrified by inequality, convinced of impending socialism, terrified of death or irritated by the fact that people aren't all the same.

The CloisterFesting process has become significantly easier with the advent of the Internet, as it provides an easy way to hook up with like-minded zealots and supplies a nearly inexhaustible source of unsubstantiated, unedited, ill-researched, sophomoric partisan drivel[3] that can be put to good use in CloisterFest activities. This boundless online fount of misinformation has made it possible for extremists to immerse themselves in wrongheaded, self-referential claptrap on an unprecedented scale.

The CloisterFest process, through its efficient delivery of overstimulation, has begun to produce some interesting behaviors among its participants. Two of these, Awareness Addiction and Outrage Buzz are briefly described below. Activist leaders have been quick to recognize the opportunities these side effects provide for keeping the flocks motivated and loyal to the cause.

A STRANGER IS JUST AN ENEMY I HAVEN'T MET.

Extremists and fringies don't know very many of the kind of people they hate/oppose, largely because of CloisterFesting. They sur-

---

3 Have you noticed that every jackass out there has published a book of political commentary these days? It's out of control, I say.

round themselves with like-minded people and invent mythologies about their opponents, which they repeat endlessly among themselves. Meeting and interacting with these "others" rarely happens, and when it does, the activist views it not as an opportunity to learn more about a different viewpoint, bridge the divide, or offer compromise, but as an opportunity to lecture, cajole, berate or firebomb the other guy.

Extremists will tell you all sorts of things about their enemies in the course of a typical tirade. Most of the information is acquired during CloisterFests or through highly biased media, books and other sources. Most of it is also wrong.[4] Nevertheless, their thoughts and actions are rooted in these incestuous mythologies, so when they patiently describe their enemies' attributes (and transgressions) to us Middles, their explanations don't reconcile with our own observations— which are based on a more broad and diverse field of information. We Middles actually know some of these people whom they are describing, and our experience rarely bears out the stereotypes they are so fond of using.

This steadfast refusal to understand their enemies creates an enormous strategic disadvantage on the political battlefield. No matter how many times they get their butts kicked by the other side, they continue to scheme against one another using ancient stereotypes and outdated information, yielding the predictable destruction-sowing stalemate. Even a plebe at a third-rate military school can tell you that you must "Know Your Enemy" if you want to be victorious.[5] Nevertheless, they simply will not learn anything about one another.

AWARENESS ADDICTION

Extremists and activists are intensely committed to the pursuit of "Awareness," and the CloisterFest is the perfect place to learn new

---

4 My first father-in-law used to do this. He would rant on about "dirty hippies" right in front of me, apparently unaware of my below-shoulder-length hair, ripped jeans, rose-tinted aviator glasses, Earth Shoes and omnipresent cannabis/nicotine/patchouli aroma.

5 I read a book called *Don't Think of an Elephant* that came out after the Kerry debacle. It was supposed to be a primer for lefties to learn to strategize "more like Republicans" during elections. It was about as helpful as an Israeli's advice on how to act "more Palestinian."

factoids and exchange anecdotes about their chosen issue. "Raising Awareness" is one of the principal activities of the extremist, and a potent source of self-esteem for the practitioner. After all, who doesn't feel better about himself when he can "educate" and "inform" dumb, apathetic, amoral or otherwise inferior people like you and me about some terribly important issue that he knows everything about and cares for deeply.

In fact, Raising Awareness often becomes more important to the activist than actually DOING anything about the problem that they are striving to make the rest of us more keenly aware of.

A hillbilly gets a scholarship to Harvard. On his first day, he encounters another student on the quad. He asks the guy:

"'Scuse me. Where's the liberry at?"

The other guy sniffs:

"Obviously you have no business at Hahvahd or you would know that one nevah ends a sentence with a preposition."

The hillbilly thinks about it for a moment, then replies:

"'Scuse me. Where's the liberry at, asshole?"

What does that have to do with the subject at hand? Nothing whatsoever. I was just reminded of it when I ended a sentence with a preposition (above). Back to the point:

One of the side effects of High Awareness is a continual craving for more and ever-higher Awareness. This addiction is similar to most others (drugs, alcohol, gambling, power, sex), except in two respects:

- Awareness addicts don't try to hide their problem. On the contrary, they are proud to constantly tell people like me how deeply Aware they are of their pet issue.

- They don't "Bogart" their Awareness drug. Far from it— they feel compelled to "share" it with the rest of us. Endlessly.

SOMEBODY SHOULD DO SOMETHING!
(How About You?)

Awareness raising is an activity that many activists engage in because it allows them to feel good about themselves without doing anything important about the problem. That "dirty work" can be conveniently left to someone else— presumably someone who learned about the Cause from the "awareness raising" activities of the aforementioned activist (Activist A, in the following example). The advantage of this strategy is that Activist A can host rallies, marches, get-togethers, parties and other social events where s/he can Inspire Others (Activists B1, B2, B3, and so on) through her/his Commitment and Leadership, so those amped-up B-level activists will join the Peace Corps, go to Zimbabwe and get shot by a 12-year-old, Kalashnikov-wielding rebel, while unloading bags of rice from a United Nations lorry.

The table below contrasts the venues, activities and experiences of the two types of activists and vividly illustrates the advantages of being an A-level player.

RAISING AWARENESS / DOING SOMETHING COMPARISON TABLE

Raising Awareness	Doing Something
Hollywood mansion	Mud hut
Parties	Civil War
Delicious Amuse-bouche	Crunchy live insects
Fine wines	Water fouled with human feces
Trendy clothes	The same clothes as last month
Publicity photo shoot	Ducking when someone shoots
Get to meet Sting	Get scorpion sting
Guest shot on Bill Maher	Supervisor shot by insurgent
Press conference to save children	Press femoral artery to save leg
Hangover	Dysentery
Unmet fund raising goals	Death

It should be obvious that Raising Awareness beats the hell out of Doing Something hands down, which is why when it comes to activism— you want to get in early. It's a lot like Amway, really.

OUTRAGE BUZZ

Outrage Buzz is a condition closely intertwined with Awareness Addiction. Once the activist becomes Fully Aware of the issue at hand, the next step, of course, is to become "Outraged" about it. Outrage is fun. It's a buzz, like rooting for the Home Team. It revs the heart rate, improves circulation, and brings a rosy glow to the cheeks. Plus, it shows the world that you and your cohorts are the only ones Paying Attention; who Really Care; who Have Morals; or Get It. Best of all, it creates a sense of solidarity among the users, making the CloisterFest, demonstration, revival, convention or retreat a memorable affair for all, priming the activist to:

THINK GLOBALLY.
OVERREACT LOCALLY.[6]

Just because YOU say the sky is falling doesn't mean it is. I realize that you just saw a Compelling Documentary on the subject, which contained a whole bunch of stuff that really got you thinking— and that you want to share this new insight with me. I appreciate that sentiment— really, I do.

But at the moment I'm trying to enjoy a too-expensive cup of coffee that I don't give a shit where it came from or who grows the beans, in a chain store that may or may not have put some mom-and-pop out of business— which I don't give a shit about, either. Now, I realize that I might come off as a callous prick to some folks, but here's how I look at it:

You, Brave Activist, don't know anything about me. You don't know whether I give half my income to the Wounded Knee Founda-

---

6 Bumper sticker available at mindyourownvote.com

tion, make kiddie-porn films for a living, run a biofuel operation, or am the local Grand Klaxtoop of the KKK. But when you invade my space to tell me about your Cause, you are making several assumptions about me that are highly insulting:

- I don't already know plenty about Your Cause.
- I'm not "doing enough" about it.
- Your Cause is more important than My Cause.
- My contribution to society is generally inadequate, although you don't know what my contribution actually is.

So, if you approach me with your little pamphlet that some wide-eyed graphic-design student produced *gratis*, and you get a response somewhere between indifference and open hostility, that's why: because the act of invading my life is offensive.

Besides, you have a vested interest in the sky falling— so you can fantasize that you're capable of fixing it. And you probably plan to blame me for the problem, too. So, please, get yourself a nice chai whatever, and sit quietly at another table reading your pamphlet for the umpteenth time. And have a nice day.

STICKS AND STONES CAN BREAK MY BONES, BUT WORDS: NOW WE'RE TALKING ABOUT REAL PAIN.

Political Correctness has been covered by many commentators in a host of interesting ways, so it's a bit cheeky, perhaps, to think I might have anything original to add— and I might not. But, shit— how can I not say something about the most-pernicious assault on free speech in modern times?

Foremost has to be the fact that PC is brought to you by the same people who devised the idea of the ACLU: an organization that will go to court to defend the right of neo-Nazis to march in a Jewish neighborhood. Political Correctness is a tool invented by the political movement whose very core— its heart-of-hearts— is purportedly the protection of people's rights against tyranny. Bizarre.

Like many pernicious evils, PC started with good intentions. And also like many pernicious evils, it turned into, well, a pernicious evil. I guess the original idea was that if we "trained" people not to say bad words, they would eventually stop thinking bad words, then eventually we'd all … uh … hmmm.

Just what the fuck was the idea, anyway?

Despite its righteous roots, Political Correctness is now used as a cudgel to randomly punish certain presumed highly-insensitive people for imagined crimes against certain other, self-identified groups of highly-sensitive people. It now serves as a revenge mechanism for people to employ against their real or imagined tormentors.

I'm not suggesting that I don't understand the desire for revenge. After all, revenge is the entire subject of this book, after you strip away all the brilliant prose and gratuitous profanity.

The trouble with PC is that it exposes a fundamental hypocrisy that underlies the Progressive Liberal philosophy. Despite all the rhetoric about Equality, what they really want is Domination— just as all their enemies do. And like every other group of people that has struggled for dominant power, they are going to settle some scores if and when they get it.

PC confers special power to a self-selected group of people— all in the name of "fairness." This power allows them to accuse anyone they choose of racist, sexist or other offensive speech and behavior, according to a secret set of rules which change continually and are never revealed unless the PC practitioner decides someone has already violated them. Because these rules are never published, they can be deduced only by inference— through the study of the alleged offenses themselves. I have taken the liberty of ordering up just such a study by my Research Department, and the preliminary results are shown below.

Many important rules, conditions, exceptions and variables apply to the proper application of PC (Note: these rules will have changed by the time you read this. We can only provide a snapshot of their state at the time of publication). Herewith, the rules of Political Correctness:

- Anyone can define, without justification, a set of attributes that constitute an Offendable Group, except White Males;

- Anyone can make themselves, without justification, a member of one or more of these Offendable Groups, except White Males;

- Anyone who is a member of an Offendable Group can define any actions, words, phrases, gestures or combination thereof as an Offensive Act;

- For an Act to be deemed Offensive, it must have been committed by someone who is not a member of the Offendable Group, because,

- Offendable Group members may use the same actions, words, phrases or gestures regarding themselves, ironically or otherwise, without penalty;

- Offendable Groups are allowed to arbitrarily define the nature and severity of any and all Offensive Acts, without regard to logic, dictionary definition, or objective truth;

- At any time, a member of an Offendable Group may redefine the nature and severity of an Offensive Act, including, if convenient, completely reversing a previously held definition;

- Contradictory rulings made by any authority such as the Supreme Court are irrelevant;

- Any observations made by GreedyWhiteMales are automatically Offensive Acts, including those unexpressed;

- Any actions, words, phrases, gestures or combination thereof made by a member of an Offendable Group toward a GreedyWhiteMale are acceptable and encouraged— even if they equal or exceed the levels of vitriol and denigration made at a Skinhead rally.

If you set yourselves out as the defenders of something like Free Speech, you need to defend everyone's right to it; including bigots, malevolent shitheads, stupid louts, and yes— even Christian white guys.

FRAMING THE DIALOGUE

Activists also love to engage the rest of us in "dialogue" about their pet issue. It's their way of "raising awareness," recruiting volunteers, and venting frustration that ignoramus Middles are ignoring them. They're pumped up about their pet subject and want to "dialogue" about it. By "dialogue," I mean "lecture," and it typically includes four important features:

- The activist/believer assumes he is going to supply all "facts," concepts, research, findings and conclusions relating to the subject.
- The activist/believer assumes he is going to define all terms[7] used in the discussion.
- The activist/believer assumes he is going to determine which aspects of the subject are "off limits."
- The activist/believer assumes he is going to do all the talking.

The "dialogue" will begin with the activist giving a snapshot of the Outrage At Hand— often noting that you, the listener, are not Properly Outraged despite the preponderance of Glaring Evidence. Next, working on the presumption that you simply don't have the appropriate Glaring Evidence to reach the Obvious Conclusion, he will "patiently" download you with a litany of "facts," "fun facts," background, supposition, mythology, misinformation, unsupportable conclusions, inane conjectures, conspiracy-theory sidebars, lies, fabrications, leaps-of-logic, false correlations, impossible causal relationships, and possibly a kernel of truth about the subject.

His mastery over the subject material will be established by quoting various prominent experts who you consider raging assholes, and

---

7 This is where you will see a lot of nounjetives, which will be explained a few pages hence.

by referencing media sources and authors that you know are utterly biased. Inevitably, the presentation will conclude with a wrap-up of which political party is at fault and the observation that no one is taking the issue seriously— particularly, people like YOU.

You— the other participant in the "dialogue" are not permitted to do any of the following:

- Point out obvious flaws in logic;
- Dispute any facts or data presented;
- Question the credentials of any of the experts quoted;
- Add data of your own;
- Suggest alternate conclusions that might be drawn from the information presented;
- Question the "seriousness" of the problem;
- Point out that someone is "already working on it";
- Suggest that a solution exists or is at hand;
- Suggest that the problem is a figment of his imagination;
- Indicate that you don't give a shit;
- Interrupt;
- Escape.

WELL, ARE YOU AN IDIOT OR AN ASSHOLE?
(Also known as the Idiot/Asshole Conundrum)

The activist will then insist that you "choose sides," operating on the presumption that the manner in which he has framed the issue is the only way to look at it. You, the Middle, face a dilemma:

- If you pretend to agree with him, he will stop the lecture, but you must compromise your principles.
- Pretending to agree will not work because you will not know enough of the necessary buzzwords and pass-phrases to carry on the conversation.

- If you disagree, he will redouble his efforts to persuade you.

- If you assert that you don't want to talk about it, that is equivalent to disagreeing, and he will redouble his efforts.

- If you choke him to death, you will get caught and do hard time.

Often, you will find yourself in a group of people representing two sides of an issue, who will argue about it until someone notices that you haven't said a word. This will piss off both groups of partisans, and they will turn on you as a common enemy. When caught in the cross-fire between oppositional activists, the Middle experiences something akin to the following:

> Activist One: "So, then, I guess you're in favor of murdering innocent baby fetuses created by God, while promoting promiscuity and irresponsible sexual activity among underage girls and unmarried women, right?"

> Activist Two: "So, then, I guess you endorse denying women control over their own bodies, allowing men to dominate them, and forcing them into a medieval choice between ruining their lives or getting dangerous back-alley abortions, right?"

> Activists One and Two, in unison: "Well, Middle, which side are you on? WHAT'S YOUR ANSWER?"

Here's my answer: Both of you can kiss my Ethiopian ass.[8] You don't have the authority to demand that I take a position either way. Just because *you* want to "dialogue" about something does not mean that:

- I want to;

- The subject is important to anyone but you;

---

8 I had my genome traced. Turns out I'm descended from some sort of protohuman from what is now Ethiopia. Who knew? All this time I thought I was some white guy. Guess what else? You're an Ethiopian, too. Word.

- Anything you think or say is accurate;
- I am in any way obligated to weigh in.
- It is any of your business what I think.

So get outta' my face.

WHY DON'T YOU JUST ADMIT YOU'RE AN IDIOT, SO WE CAN MOVE PAST THIS?

Only one small impediment prevents an all-out pandemic of bipartisan cooperation in this country: and that is the insistence by each group that the other simply make one teeny-tiny, little concession that will make it possible to "work together as Americans toward our shared goal of Universal Whatever, blah, blah." That doesn't seem like too much to ask, does it?

That niggling[9] little concession is the demand that, as a condition of future dialogue, the other side simply concede that their world view is morally bankrupt, venal, bigoted, selfish or some version of "completely wrongheaded." Both sides do this, and no matter how dismally the technique fails to produce results other than increased animosity, they still cling to it.

I think they like it that way because it avoids the frightening possibility of actually having a meaningful exchange of ideas, which, if it were to occur, might require that someone's point of view be changed, or worse, could precipitate the discovery that one was in fact WRONG.

I witnessed this kind of exchange between two partisans— one Red, one Blue. The subject was Global Warming and the combatants could not get past the issue of whether humankind was responsible for the increasing global temperatures. The Red Stater didn't think human activity was the cause, and the Blue Stater believed it was unequivocal, so they battled like rutting stags for an hour until the argument dissolved into animosity.

---

9 This is not a racial slur.

Keep in mind that they agreed to the following points:

- Temperatures seem to be, in fact, rising,
- The general time frame of the effect is roughly coincident with Industrialization, and,
- We ought to do something about it.

This did not provide enough common ground to "hug it out." Despite agreement on all the salient points necessary to form an action plan, they still wanted to fight to the finish over the issue of causation.[10] That's because neither could see nor admit that they were really arguing about something else. The Blue Stater was frustrated and angry about having explained this to bullheaded Red Staters a million times over, yet still No One Is Listening. The Red Stater, on the other hand, was tired of being lectured by Blue Staters about everything that's wrong with society (read: Red-State society) and, by insinuation, being blamed for the problems.

So, in this case, the entire argument hinged on the term "human activity," which is, of course, a heavily loaded, pejorative political code term for "your activity," if the person wielding the term:

- is already "off the grid";
- has a brochure about how to get "off the grid";
- knows someone who lives in a yurt, "off the grid"; or
- has seen Al Gore's film.

Under these circumstances, there is no way to have a discussion of carbon reduction because the issue of blame is in the way, and you, as the "human activity-ist," need to cover your ass.[11]

It doesn't need to be so complicated. We could gather every stakeholder in the warming debate and allow them to argue until the methane-

---

10 Blame.

11 If you are a Blue-state secular humanist or other form of Sinner, the process is reversed— although the issue will not be Global Warming. Instead, you will be confronted by some sort of "born-again" believer, requiring that you spend your energy defending yourself against implied accusations of immorality.

emitting cows come home, and when they are finished howling at one other, here is the three-stage action plan that will need to be implemented, as soon as possible:

1) **Reduce the living shit out of carbon emissions from:**
- cars and trucks;
- trains, planes and ships;
- farming and livestock production;
- plastics manufacturing;
- building materials manufacturing;
- energy extraction, production and distribution; and,
- everything else that emits carbon that I haven't thought of.

2) **Reduce the living shit out of:**
- electricity consumption;
- fuel consumption;
- food consumption;
- water consumption;
- forest consumption;
- mineral consumption; and,
- world population growth.

3) **Get world leaders to "work together" (HA!) to:**
- there's no point in finishing this section, obviously;
- just pray for the Killer Comet.

Nevertheless, we could start working on everything on the first two sections of this list without ever deciding who is to blame. But that's not enough for America's two primary political enemies. Neither would savor anything more than to be able to say "I told you so" to the other group— even if we all have to go up in smoke so they can enjoy that magic sanctimonious moment.

So, although the debate is ostensibly about "global warming," "race relations," "our education system," "sex on TV," or whatever, it's really a proxy for our ongoing class war. And in America's class war, it's mandatory that someone concedes that they are at fault before we can all move to the next subject, which is:

What in the hell are we going to do about it?

Evidently, it bothers no one if we never get to that part.

Part Five:

TOOLS AND TACTICS

Now that we have our "positions" nicely verbalized, let's move on to the process of shoving them through the alimentary canal of American discourse. Below, I will describe some artificial-dissemination techniques that Activists use to move misinformation from stage to minds and hearts, in the grand theater of American politics.

GREEDYCAPITALIST: THE BIRTH OF THE NOUNJETIVE

Through CloisterFesting, political debate, and intellectual laziness, a new style of terminology has been created: what I call the Nounjetive.

Nounjetives are formed when particular terms are used together so often that they become fused, inseparably, in the mind of the user. For example, the noun "Capitalist" (a person engaged in the sale of goods and services for financial gain), has been merged with the adjective "Greedy" (interested in monetary or other gain without regard to ethics, morals, unintended victims, social justice) to fledge a new term: "GreedyCapitalist."

For the frequent user, just as the adjective has collapsed into the noun, the ideas behind the words have also fused, to create— in this example— a new definition of capitalism as inseparable from greed. Just as a "nonbeliever" is by religious definition a "sinner," a "capitalist" is now, by liberal definition, "greedy." This new mind-set functions as a filtering device for all information received regarding the subject of free enterprise, resulting in a group of people who hate capitalism without knowing one accurate thing about it.

In his book *Empire of Illusion*, Chris Hedges casually tosses out an indictment of capitalism while discussing the effects of celebrity culture and spectacle programming (such as professional wrestling and Reality TV) upon the minds and morals of its consumers. He is discussing the false alliances, duplicity, subterfuge and betrayal exhibited by members of the cast of the TV hit *Survivor*, and how these behaviors mirror our celebrity culture at large. He writes:

Celebrity culture plunges us into a moral void. No one has any worth beyond his or her appearance, usefulness, or ability to "succeed." The highest achievements in a celebrity culture are wealth, sexual conquest, and fame. It does not matter how these are obtained. These values …

… urge us toward a life of narcissistic self-absorption. They tell us that existence is to be centered on the practices and desires of the self rather than the common good.

So far; so good. I'm behind him at this point, and thoroughly enjoying the book. Then comes the next sentence:

The ability to lie and manipulate others, the very ethic of capitalism, is held up as the highest good.

The very ethic of capitalism. His point about celebrity culture would have been sufficiently made without this phrase and, worse, he offers it up as an undisputed fact— without evidence or discussion. If someone made a similar sweeping generality about, say, Native Americans, women or third-world countries, you wouldn't be able to hear yourself think over all the howling protest.

He is, of course, free to think anything he wants about capitalism or any other subject. However, these types of throwaway lines are used by politicians, journalists, believers and extremists so often that no one even wastes the effort to challenge them any more.

Now, I realize that Political Correctness has stripped us of most of our traditional Bad Guys: Injuns; Eye-talians; Chinamen; Savages— hell, even the Nazis (for fear of opening old wounds among contemporary Germans) are often off-limits. There's probably some group out there fighting against the defamation of Boogeymen.[1]

As a result, within the literary/screenwriting/political mythmaking milieu, we're pretty much left with Terrorists, Aliens (from space, not Mexico), Communism (snore) and Capitalism.

---

1 To join the Boogeyman Anti-Defamation League (BADF), go to mindyourownvote.com.

In the US, capitalism is an easy and popular target of malicious criticism for a number of reasons:

- Poor people can blame it for all their misery;

- Rich people can blame it for the plight of their poverty-stricken moral mascots;

- Hippies can feel morally superior for living in a yurt somewhere;

- Environmentalists can blame all pollution, loss of habitat, degradation and warming on it;

- Liberal writers can use it as a metaphor for any evil;

- Everyone can hate the oligarchy that stokes the engines of it;

- The oligarchy couldn't care less how much you hate it, so you are free to say whatever you want without the repercussions that would result if you defamed any other group of people in a similar manner.

Talk about a free lunch.

As I was writing this, the Occupy Wall Street movement was in full swing ("We're going to play these conga drums until you, uh... hmmm... —We're not kidding here— if you don't... wha? Those rich bastards are flying right over us in their helicopters! Hey, assholes!— Down here! We demand our fair share!!!) and thousands of disgruntled people are demanding we create more jobs by shutting down capitalist enterprises.

Let's quickly review some of the organizations that rely on capitalism and its "very ethic— the ability to lie and manipulate others," to operate successfully:

- Organic farmers market
- Medical marijuana dispensary
- Conga drum manufacturer

- Occult book store
- Chris Hedges and his publisher
- Head shop
- Independent coffee shop
- Artist collective
- Alternative rock musicians
- Bono
- Liberal activist actors
- Michael Moore
- *The Huffington Post*
- The Democratic Party
- Those are just the ones I thought of without getting another aneurysm

Hey, while we're on the subject of Ruthless, Predatory Capitalistic Monoliths, why are all you left-wing, hippie dopers out there supporting one of the most-ruthless of them all: the drug cartels? Just wondering.

Boy, did I get off track.

Anyway, this penchant for forming Nounjetives persists on both sides of the political divide and has created a lexicon of highly descriptive, deeply biased, colorful terms that have been adopted by everyone engaging in political discourse, particularly the media.

A short list of collapsed terms:

- TaxAndSpendLiberal
- GreedyCorporation
- ObstructionistRepublican
- RedStateIdiot
- BedwettingLiberal
- LiberalElite

- GreedyWhiteMale
- PersonalResponsibility
- KneeJerkLiberal
- EvilDrugCompanies
- FairShare
- ExcessProfits
- HardWorkingAmericans
- UnderappreciatedUnderpaidTeachers
- StrugglingArtist
- NeedyChildren
- AngryFeminist
- ManHatingFeminist
- LesbianFeminist
- FemiNazi

I have no doubt that you can think of many more. For further study, watch The O'Reilly Factor, Hannity sans Colmes, consult The *Huffington Post* or pick up any college textbook on any subject.

THE POWER OF STATISTICS

The science of statistics is a powerful tool used by all participants in the American political process— especially Activists. One of the most-important functions of statistics is to determine precisely how, and to what degree, you can claim that you and your constituents are being screwed by the system. This data can then be used to great effect in campaign advertising and speech making.

Fortunately for politicians and others with a cause to promote, 97.4% of all Americans[2] believe that the entire field of mathematics

---

2 See how easy it is? There's a statistic already!

is boring, nerdish and irrelevant. Accordingly, few Americans[3] have even a rudimentary grasp of the science of statistics, and will believe all claims that support their cherished point of view, while rejecting all others.

This indifference to mathematics— or anything to do with any numbers that are not related to sports— is also why Americans will buy houses, cars, ATV's, foosball tables, lap-dances and other stuff they can't afford, and be completely comfortable paying 22% interest on the cost of those items while inhabiting a nation that operates its federal budget in the same way.

But I digress.[4]

Statistics— the most malleable of the mathematics subspecialties— is particularly handy for anyone promoting a political agenda for several reasons:

- No one can tell if your statistics are true or false;

- If you can manage to get any form of media to quote your statistic, it will be instantly broadcast around the globe as an Unassailable Fact, arriving in every American voter's e-mail inbox and/or Twitter feed within two minutes.

- Statistics can be used to prove a point— and it's opposite— at the same time, a particularly useful aspect if you can steal your opponent's hard-won and expensive research before publication, and use it against her/him.

Meanwhile, let us explore how The Science of Statistics yields these magical properties. Below is a simple example of the process of manufacturing statistics.

---

3 Asians, however, emerge from the womb fully conversant in statistics, as well as multivariable and stochastic calculus, Boolean logic, string theory, and 12-dimensional particle physics. They use Boze-Einstein condensates as paperweights. As a result, statistical trickery does not work as effectively on them. Keep this in mind when trying to bamboozle this constituency.

4 You should be getting used to this by now.

First, we must collect some Raw Data.

Raw Data:

- Three years ago, one Uzbek was denied equal housing in your city.
- Two years ago, two Uzbeks were denied equal housing in your city.
- Last year, two Uzbeks were denied equal housing in your city.
- This year, one Uzbek was denied equal housing in your city.

Next, we analyze the Raw Data to look for Trends and Relationships among the various pieces (known individually as "Datum"[5]), so we can arrive at an Hypothesis about what Meaning is Revealed by the Data. Once formulated, this "Hypothesis" is immediately transformed into a "Fact"[6] and distributed to all concerned parties in the form of the dreaded PowerPoint® presentation.[7] These facts can then be employed to prove or refute any assertion. Back to our example:

Partial list of Factual Results (all the following statements are true, according to the data supplied above):

- Housing discrimination against Uzbeks is 600% higher than three years ago.
- The rate of housing discrimination against Uzbeks has dropped by half in the last year.

---

5 This is one reason the Roman Empire is no longer around. The singular— datum, is longer than the plural— data. It doesn't take a rocket scientist to see that this is precisely backward. If they failed to notice this, who knows what else they missed? There weren't, however, any rocket scientists back then (not in Rome, anyway— the Chinese had 'em), so maybe that explains it.

6 No energy or mass is either created or lost in this transformation. This phenomenon is known as the Franken-Limbaugh Conversion Conundrum, and helps explain the rich sustainability of Statistics as a science.

7 It is now possible, evidently, to make an Oscar-worthy movie by videotaping a PowerPoint presentation and charging for attendance. This will be eagerly attended by the same people who, while at work, will do ANYTHING to get out of attending a PowerPoint presentation.

- The number of housing discrimination incidents against Uzbeks this year is 1/5 of the aggregate for the previous three years.
- Currently there are three Uzbek housing discrimination victims in your city for every one victim three years ago.
- There is only one Uzbek housing discrimination victim this year for every two victims two years ago.

These "Factual Results" can next be translated into Political Capital by simply adding an Implied[8] Causal Relationship, and the result is known as a "Statistic."

- Because of the valiant and selfless efforts of the volunteers of the Uzbek Anti-Housing Discrimination Association and the implementation of its brave campaign against City Hall, the rate of housing discrimination against Uzbeks has plummeted 50% this year alone.
- Despite the valiant efforts of the Uzbek Anti-Housing Discrimination Association to educate our bull-headed representatives at City Hall, discrimination against Uzbeks has risen by a shocking 600% in just three short years.

See how much fun statistics can be? Once you and your aggrieved group get a good handle on statistics, you can prove your victimhood even if nothing bad has actually happened to you!

Who says math is dry as toast?

---

8 False, in other words.

PROBABILITY:
YOU PROBABLY DON'T UNDERSTAND IT.

Most Americans do not understand probability statistics, which is unfortunate because politicians and extremist groups love to use them to confuse the public. For example, what does it mean when your favorite newspaper reports:

> "Americans are three times as likely to be victims of victimization than they were when the previous victimization rate was one-third of its present level."[9]

Who can tell? I don't understand probabilities very well either, but I do know several important things that can be valuable aids in evaluating probability statistics, however baffling. These simple rules may be helpful in evaluating probabilities that you may encounter in the future and I present them here as a public service.[10]

JC's Rules of Probability:

The likelihood that you have overestimated your ability to understand probabilities is higher than you think.
The ramifications of this rule are devilishly complex because probability theory is deeply counterintuitive, and most of us don't want to admit that we can't grasp something. The rule suggests that you should expect to be fooled by probability statistics, and guard against this by being more skeptical. However, because you cannot accurately estimate the probability of being fooled, you are likely to incorrectly determine the quantity of compensatory skepticism to apply in each case— probably undercompensating in the process. So if you hear a probability claim that "sounds about right" or "makes sense to me"— you should assume it sounds plausible because you don't, in fact, "get it." Get it?

---

9 This is either a logical syllogism or a tautology— or not.

10 I'm a friggin' saint, wouldn't you agree?

The only safe bet is to become deeply and permanently skeptical, despite the knowledge that you're probably overcompensating.

Nearly every probability statistic you will ever hear in your life will be presented by someone with an agenda that involves getting you to do something.

This means that you will rarely be provided the "big picture" information that will put the probability in context; in other words— the critical information that can allow you to translate meaningless snippets of data into actual knowledge. Probabilities are used by partisans to scare us into believing just about anything. The safe bet in this case is to assume that the truth is the opposite of whatever the partisan is saying.

Probability data regarding past events is useless for predicting the future, although everyone employs it for just that purpose.

Think about it: have you ever seen any data that would have predicted the emergence of the following?:

- Emo music and fashion;

- Paris Hilton, Britney Spears, Lady Gaga et al;

- Second Life;[11]

- Hillary becoming "uncool" in the course of two months;

- The Arab world spontaneously erupting into demands for democracy;

- Rupert Murdoch being torn apart by the media;

- LifeCasting;[12]

---

11 This seems particularly ironic as a name, because if you had a First Life, you wouldn't be there.

12 This is, uh, where you are an oversexed, underdressed 17-year-old girl, and you make videos about yourself and put them up on the web for every pervert to jerk off to. Subjects covered include the salad you had for lunch, the appearance of zits at inconvenient times, video of you puking into a public toilet, and other material that you want a future mate, employer, etc. to be able to view later in your life. This occurs far less often than in years past because of the arrival of social media such as Facebook, where everyone is basically lifecasting—not just the exhibitionists.

- Oval-office blow jobs;
- FaceBook, AssBook,[13] Plinky, Plurk;
- Texting, Twittering, Jaiku, etc.;
- "Sexting"[14]

FACT-BASHING

Once so artfully produced, what do the partisan nutjobs do with these "facts" that are generated by the Statistical Method?

They bash us with 'em!

This is the final phase of the statistics-manufacturing process, and where all the effort finally pays off. But first, the statistics need to be organized. You can't have a big pile of them just lying about willy-nilly. No sirree— they need to be fitted into your "Platform," so you can use them as ammunition in the "Dialogue" process. Here's how that works:

First, the statistics need to be ranked according to their potential power to persuade, so they are sorted into "shock-value" classes based on the "Sky-Is-In-Fact-Falling" (SIIFF) scale shown below:

Appalling
Disturbing
Troubling
Slippery-slope confirming
"Worrisome-trend" starting
Thought-provoking
Concerning
Inconvenient

---

13 Yes, there really is such a thing, and, yes, it's pretty much what it sounds like.

14 For the uninitiated, sexting is a procedure where you send photos of your tits, booty, wanger (or Weiner, in the contemporary version), etc. to others, using your digital handheld device (phone, for you older folks), for the purposes of "hooking up" (getting laid, for you older folks). This runs completely counter to the intuitions of every previous generation in human history— which employed the tactic of hiding these body parts until it was, essentially, Too Late.

There will, of course, be a number of the freshly discovered/revealed facts that are essentially neutral ("nothing new", "obvious", "self-evident") that will be combined with another group of facts that are contradictory to the activist's political position ("blasphemous," "irritating," "inconvenient"). These two groups of facts will be compiled into a separate report and thrown in the trash (after being shredded).

Next, the remaining, shock-categorized facts will be disseminated in the form of speeches, press conferences, blogs, catechisms, pamphlets, talk radio, protest signs, late-night "comedy-talk" shows, newscasts, magazines, newspapers,[15] tweets, texts, and personally hurled invective— during "dialogue."

None of this will have any persuasive effect on discourse, because the Opposition is already armed with the other half of the sorting mechanism: the Partisan Factoid Dismissal Index, which exactly counteracts the power contained in the inbound statistic. The PFDI looks like this:

Arguable
Unlikely
Dubious
Laughable
Ludicrous
Irresponsible
Dangerous
Preposterous

Refutation is a simple process of cross-matching the shock value of the statistic with the corresponding dismissal term on the combined SIIFF/PFDI grid, as shown the following page:

---

15 A form of communication consisting of words and pictures, in mostly black "ink," on big sheets of rough white paper. In the past these were delivered directly to your front porch by underpaid, oppressed child laborers, a fact which the media chose to ignore despite the obvious hypocrisy.

SIIFF/PFDI STATISTIC-NEUTRALIZING GRID

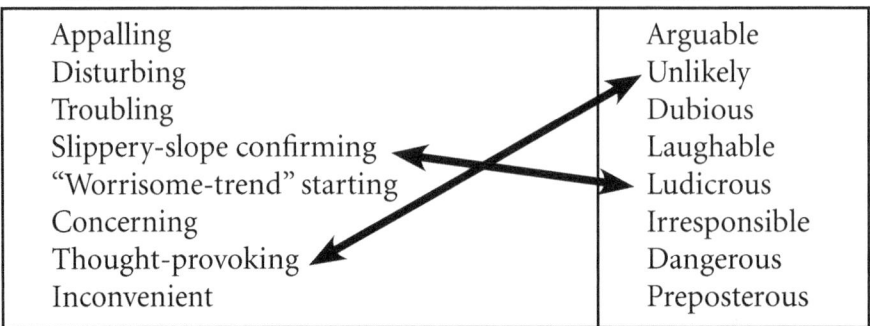

Appalling	Arguable
Disturbing	Unlikely
Troubling	Dubious
Slippery-slope confirming	Laughable
"Worrisome-trend" starting	Ludicrous
Concerning	Irresponsible
Thought-provoking	Dangerous
Inconvenient	Preposterous

The net result of this process is that the quality of intellectual discourse is not improved one *iota*— despite all the time, energy, money, and political capital expended by both groups.

Speaking of speeches, press conferences, blogs, catechisms, pamphlets, talk radio, protest signs, late-night "comedy-talk" shows, newscasts, magazines, newspapers, tweets, texts, and personally hurled invective …

Part Six:

SCHMOLITICS

For Activists and True Believers, many facets of life are imbued with political meaning. Some extremists believe that everything is political. This includes: what you eat, wear and consume; where you got it and how it got there; how you got the money to pay for it; what you read, watch and listen to; the words you use and how you use them; what we teach (and don't teach) our children; how much energy you consume and who made money in the process; where you stick your pecker and whether or not you have one; and everything else you do and think— including whether you even should have the right to do and think it in the first place.

A disturbing number of these people are our elected representatives.

POLITICIANS, AGENTS OF (OUCH!) CHANGE

Politicians raise millions of dollars and run exhausting campaigns so they can go to Washington. They don't go there for the purpose of doing nothing whatsoever (OK, a few do). They go there to "make change."[1] Their core philosophy rests on the idea that change is good and stasis is bad (this is true for Conservative politicians despite their reputation. They go to Washington to repeal legislation enacted by Liberals).

Politicians are people who would decide that San Diego's weather should be "improved," and write legislation to make it more like Honolulu's. The *San Diego Weather Improvement Act* would, of course, be a typically poorly conceived and implemented work— riddled with inadequate definitions, ambiguous regulations, inane review policies and ruinous penalties. Due to the inevitable unintended consequences, implementation of the Act would result in San Diego's weather turning out just like Seattle's. Regardless, they would declare the whole thing a stunning success, and immediately implement the same policy in Santa Barbara.

---

1 I think we would all be better off if they were "making change" at Wal-Mart instead.

The reason they do obviously dumb things such as this is because they are Agents of Change, and, as such, must (drum roll ...):

Change Stuff.

Agents of Change often position themselves as "Progressive," so if you oppose them, you can be labeled "backward" or "stodgy." Alternatively, they can position themselves as "Fundamentalist," so if you oppose them, you can be labeled "immoral" or "perverted."

The politician's *raison d'être*[2] is to write legislation, add to statutory code, broker deals, make pork, wield influence, negotiate compromises, and/or command in a "Chief-like" manner.

Because politicians are change agents, you will never hear the following campaign promise:

My fellow Americans ...

... when I look around this great nation of ours, I don't see anything that can't be fixed without my brilliant insight and dazzling prowess. You seem to be doing a great job all by yourselves. Beats the hell out of me how you do it without a degree from Georgetown, but the evidence is impossible to ignore. Elect me and I will go to Washington and do everything in my power to ensure that you can live your lives unmolested, at least for the eight consecutive terms that I plan to hold this office. This is my solemn vow.

This is also why Libertarians can rarely get elected. What are they supposed to campaign about: all the things they're *not* going to do when they get to Washington? If a candidate announces a Town Hall meeting to describe the ways he's going to leave us the hell alone, why show up? Who needs the *details* of a plan for being left unmolested?

Back to the point.

---

2 French. Employed to make the author appear classically educated and erudite. Not sure what it means or whether I've employed it appropriately.

Middles don't want someone messing around with life's operating system all the time. We're not Early Adopters. We don't care if we have Social Reconstruction Version 3,456.34.5.7 alpha or Version 3,456.34.5.7 beta. We would just ask that everyone stop reinstalling the OS so we can get some friggin' work done. The Socialist vision imposed on us by the Blue Team is, on balance, no better or worse than the Fundamentalist one imposed by the Red Team. They both suck, but we can make do, as we always have. It's all the "imposing," "reimposing" and "counter-imposing" that's such a huge pain in the ass.

So what happens? All these people with unattainable ideals go to the City Council, State House, White House or Condominium Association and work out compromises that include the worst features of each idealist's vision, then sign it into law and foist it on the rest of us. Then they start over, and because they're Idealists, this horrible process goes on forever.

I flunked math several times, but one item I did manage to pick up was the concept that there are an infinite number of points on a line, and that between each point is sufficient room for another infinite number of points, *ad infinitum*.[3] This has huge implications for the Writing of Policy, as shown here:

- Regardless of the level of detail that is written into a given policy, law, regulation, clarification, restatement, amendment and/or addendum, there is still the potential for an infinite amount of additional detail between each adjacent existing detail.

This serves two important functions:

- To provide permanent employment for lawmakers, and,

- To provide a permanent supply of loopholes for violators.

This system works brilliantly for politicians because people who write policy are abysmally bad at closing all the gaps in the policy they write, and, conversely, people who want to break the rules are aston-

---

3 I'm not certain whether this was Algebra or Geometry, but the concept is still vivid nonetheless. Plus, I might have made a pun in Latin. Also not certain.

ishingly good at locating those gaps and driving a train through them. Think junk bonds, welfare scams, environmental policy, subprime mortgages, bailouts, cap-and-trade, military spending, congressional oversight— you get the idea.

It's a beautiful, self-sustaining cycle: politicians write inadequate policy; violators take advantage of the loopholes; politicians use the violators' behavior to get elected on a reform ticket; they write additional inadequate policy, and the process repeats. Job security for politicians and violators alike.

POLITICAL PARTIES

Our political system is based on the Two-Party system:

Our Party, and

Their Party.

Our Political Party is a group of thoughtful, involved, caring, patriotic individuals dedicated to important causes such as the pursuit of happiness, the well-being of our fellow citizens, equal justice under the law, continually growing economic prosperity, compassion for those less fortunate and the enjoyment of maximum liberty for everyone. We are what makes America great.

Their Political Party is a group of selfish, partisan, greedy, morally bankrupt idiots bent on screwing anyone who is not a member of their self-righteous, snotty elitist group, and who don't care about anyone else's needs, rights or aspirations. They are destroying everything that makes America great.

It is your civic duty as an American to join one of these parties and participate in denouncing 50% of your fellow citizens utilizing misleading advertising, unsubstantiated blog rants, lies, misquotes, invective, insults, vitriol, disparagement, harassment, proselytizing, caustic talk-radio call-ins, partisan web sites and other forms of "free speech."

Because you are joining a political party, it is not necessary to:

- learn anything about the assholes in "Their Party";
- listen to anything they might have to say;
- consider their viewpoint valid in any manner or detail;
- allow them equal time, or;
- respect their rights as citizens.

All that matters is that members of "Our Party" get elected to every level of government, however insignificant.

There is also— once you dig down deep— only one platform that our political parties put forth each election cycle, and that is this:

> Our party should get another crack at it, even though we have screwed it up every time we've tried it so far. We are not going to do anything fundamentally different from our previous attempts. However, this time we are predicting a stunning success, primarily because we have a new candidate who has some trivial characteristics that we are pretending are deeply significant.

Nevertheless, once the candidates from "Our Party" take office, they will enact legislation designed to screw "Their Party" as much as possible, while looking out for the interests of "Our Party" even if it is bad for the country as a whole.

Through this process of alternating revenge hazings, we accumulate a Sacred Body of Law that, remarkably, manages to screw almost everyone significantly more than half the time.

The important thing to remember about our political system is that no one really gives a shit about the welfare of the country that made it possible for us all to be the narcissistic, self-referential, greedy jerks that we are. It's all— and only— about winning.

ONE NATION, ONE ISSUE

A simple way to make the political process easier for yourself, eliminating the need, for example, to perform the hard and continual work necessary to be well informed— is to employ what is known as the Litmus Test. This technique gets its moniker from an otherwise-inconsequential late-nineteenth-century politician named Harold Litmus who was known for his ability, when asked any question in front of an audience, to change the subject— in the first few words of his answer— back to the single thing he wanted to talk about. No one remembers anything that he ever said— only that there was just one subject he would ever address. The foremost practitioner of this technique today is Jesse Jackson.

> Larry King: "Jesse, I understand you just returned from vacation in Gstaad, where paparazzi photographed you naked in a hot tub with three underage members of the Lithuanian Women's Ski Team, which was in town training for the Olympics."

> Jesse Jackson: "Well, Larry, 'vacation' has always meant suffering for the black man in America, because on the plantation, there was no vacation. It was toil and sweat from dawn to dusk. It's time we rectified this glaring inequity once and for all. Reparations wouldn't be a bad idea either"

> Larry King: "Actually, I was asking about the underage girls. That seems inappro …"

> Jesse Jackson: "What is inappropriate, Larry, is innocent black children being born into bondage. For fourteen generations, blacks have …"

Using the Litmus Test, you can simplify your entire approach to political participation. Let's say that you have a strong stand on reproductive rights, gun control, or the death penalty. All you need to do is determine which party supports your side of your Litmus Test Issue, go to the voting booth and punch a straight party ticket.[4] It makes no difference if your party is going to screw the country upside down and sideways on taxes, civil rights, privacy, economic reform, press freedom or whatever— all that matters is that your pet issue is protected. All the mistaken policy positions, pork spending, special-interest paybacks, lies and false promises that accompany your party platform are just, as they say in military parlance, collateral damage. So don't let it bother you.

YOUR CANDIDATE SUCKS.

This is the one (and possibly only) universal truth of American politics. You can get a bumper sticker with this slogan, leave it on your car for the rest of your life, and it will always be timely and accurate.[5] This idea could, in fact, revolutionize political discourse. If nothing else, it certainly would make it less time-consuming:

"Your candidate sucks."

"Yeah, well your candidate sucks, too."

"Can't argue with that."

"Hmmm… Think there's anyplace around here where we can get a beer and watch the game?"

"Sure, there's a joint right around the corner. It's the only place left in America where you can still get your fries cooked in beef tallow."

"No shit? Let's go."

Why does "your candidate suck"? Because your candidate is a politician, which means that your candidate is a pompous, interfering,

---

4 In some parts of the country, you can do this by pulling one lever on the voting machine. It's comforting to know that the Election Department encourages careful consideration of each ballot issue.

5 These, and other witty commentary, are available for purchase on my web site: mindyourownvote.com

oppositional, self-righteous, bullheaded doofus who can't be successful in a merit-based environment, such as the Private Sector.[6]

It also means that your candidate belongs to one of our two parties, which requires the adoption of some form of fundamental hypocrisy such as representing the interests of both overpaid, unionized working American citizens and underpaid, exploited illegal immigrants at the same time. Or being Pro-life and supporting capital punishment.

PARTY LOYALTY:
OUR WAY OR THE WHOREWAY

There's a problem with the logic of party loyalty. It doesn't stand to reason that one group of people can have the right philosophy, strategies, and answers all the time. Political parties— like all large, consensus-based organizations— are massive, inertial and slow to change.[7] Committees must be formed, platforms proposed, votes taken and input considered before an action plan can be formulated. Next, dissenters must be swayed, mollified and/or destroyed, tasks must be assigned, results interpreted, revised plans presented, etc., *ad nauseum.*

Reality doesn't have those constraints. It goes about its business of change, randomness and unpredictability without needing to reach any sort of consensus. Consequently, no party can possibly be the best prepared to cope with all events, all the time. That *any* party is *ever* prepared to deal with them at all is a miracle by itself.

A political party is a committee. Committees cannot create anything. At best, they are benign, at worst, destructive. Between these two endpoints also fall: wasteful, obstructionist, inane, slow, discrimi-

---

6 This stereotype does not apply to any politician who would like to endorse my book. In that case, I will avow to have known you for years and attest that you are a truly selfless public servant.

7 Unless a dynamic and exciting new candidate appears. Then, the party will stampede to sidle up to the new guy, trampling any policies, positions and/or loyal participants who might get in the way. Just ask Hillary. In one short election cycle, the Democratic party changed its posture from "America just might be ready for a woman in the White House" to one where a viable female candidate wasn't edgy enough because she was white and too old.

natory, larcenous, incestuous and a host of other negative outcomes. Committees have brought us the Inquisition, HUAC, Gerrymandering, political correctness, Japanese-American internment, income tax, the lynching of judicial candidates, the lynching of citizens, destroyed careers, baffling laws and regulations, moral degradation, environmental spoiling and innumerable other evils. But never mind all that. Just fill out the form below, and you won't need to think about any of that crap ever again.

PARTY-LOYALTY FORM

I, _____, am a member of the (check one):

__ Democratic __ Republican   party.

As such, I believe that the (name of party checked above) Party is solely and uniquely qualified to:

- Properly manage all the affairs of local, State, and Federal government;
- Create educational policy, and curriculum, for all our children;
- Provide for the care and well-being of all our citizens including those who will arrive in the future from wherever they might come from, including other planets and galaxies;
- Provide moral guidance for all citizens, immigrants, illegal aliens and visitors;
- Determine fairness and equity for all the people all the time;
- Exercise superpower influence over the rest of the world whether the rest of the world is interested or not;
- Enact, repeal, modify, ignore, distort, or corrupt any public policy as we see fit, regardless of changing circumstances, unseen events, disaster, catastrophe, etc.;
- Envision, plan and execute all short-, medium-, and long-term strategic visions for our citizens and, by example, everyone else in the world;
- Cope with all unforeseen events; natural, man-made, cosmic, imaginary, hysterical, demented, megalomaniacal or otherwise;
- Accurately and properly comprehend, evaluate and manage anything else that we haven't thought of, or that can't be envisioned.

I believe this because those of us in the (name of party checked above) Party have all the answers and always will. Oh! — and if I can be perpetually happy and get everything I want, that would be great, too. I'm pretty sure that's the government's job, isn't it?

Further, members of the (name of party not checked above) Party are all self-interested, corrupt, delusional idiots who are incapable of seeing the Truth, and are going to destroy our Very Way of Life, primarily because they are so goddam stubborn. Those people should never be allowed to run anything because, as I've already pointed out, everyone with a good idea is a member or the (name of party checked above) Party. Those other people are dangerous and un-American. We don't care about them. In fact, we in the (name of party checked above) Party wish members of the (name of party not checked above) Party would all just move to Canada, but of course they won't.

Signature_____

Date_____

THE GOOD SHIP BIPARTISANSHIP:
QUICK, LOWER THE LIFEBOATS.

Politicians love to talk about bipartisanship. Every election cycle, the winner blathers on about "working together," "we're all Americans," and "reaching across the aisle." It's bullshit. They want to annihilate one other. There's only one significant accomplishment in recent political memory for which our elected leaders can take true bipartisan credit: the destruction of the economy. Congratulations Gentlemen and Ladies of Government— nice work!

THE COMMITTEE PROCESS
There's just got to be a pony in here, somewhere.

Statistically, everyone is going to be wrong about half the time.[8] However, in a committee, all wrong ideas have the power to negate any correct ideas. Conversely, correct ideas have hardly any ability to overpower wrong ones. Hence, it takes a committee only a short time to stomp the life out of a good idea and replace it with a terrible one.

---

8 That's if you're doing rather well, in fact.

Actually, the term "idea" is misleading in this case. The result is more of a conglomeration of the worst aspects of each of the bad ideas proffered, because everyone on the committee gives up what they don't care about and fights like hell for their pet detail.

LESS IS MORE— LOTS MORE.

The committee process creates the worst possible outcomes by employing a technique that I have named Additive Subtraction. In this process, each committee member advocates for the removal of the most-plausible, most potentially effective, or most reasonable parts of each of the proposals under consideration (a.k.a.: "Not my idea"), while simultaneously championing the most irrational, wrongheaded, and/or laughable ones (a.k.a.: "My idea").

Each committee member then exercises the right to declare one item a "deal-breaker," and by the time the closing gavel strikes, EVERY-THING of potential value that has been brought before the committee has been stripped from consideration. This process of compiled deletions results in a body of information that is larger and more complex than any of the original proposals— yet is composed entirely of random detritus. It is then assembled into a resolution, action plan, recommendation of further study, bill, regulation or law.

During this process, we get only two very narrow points of view because there are typically only two groups of people who ever weigh in on a given subject:

- Proponents

- Detractors

This might appear at first to be a statement of such obviousness that it is bordering on stupid. But there are quite a few people missing from the debate, many of whom might have something important— perhaps even crucial— to contribute. Included in this list of missing participants are people who:

- Didn't hear about the debate in the first place;
- Are busy doing things like keeping the buses running, stocking the produce department, nursing sick children, applying nail jewelry, etc.;
- Might point out the obvious flaws in either or both positions;
- Were intentionally not invited because:
  - of their propensity for asking hard questions;
  - they are going to be tasked with the actual work involved in implementing the proposal;
  - they are going to be the most affected by the ramifications of the proposal;
  - they are going to have to pay for what is being proposed.

That any or all of these players ("stakeholders" in Proposalisian) are missing during the crucial part of the process does not bother any of the activists who are involved in the debate. In fact, all the better, as far as they are concerned. They consider those "others" to be ill-informed, unenlightened, passionless drones who don't deserve a voice anyway.

STOP ME IF YOU'VE ALREADY HEARD THIS ONE...
(Myths about the American Presidency)

Every four years in America, we endure a deeply irritating ritual in which we subject ourselves to two years of lies and promises from our presidential candidates. The promises are always the same, and always false. One of the reasons they are so obviously lies is because the candidates keep promising to do things that the Presidency is either not authorized to do, or is incapable of accomplishing because of the morass of our political system. Below are some promises that a President probably cannot deliver:

"I will create jobs."

"I will keep jobs from going overseas."

"I will reform the schools."[9]

"I will lower fuel prices."

"I will end Global warming."[10]

"I will close the borders."

"I will defeat terrorism."

"I will get health care for every American."

"I will get rid of special-interest in government."

I love that last one. What kind of interest ISN'T a "special interest"? Labor? Conservation? Business? Education? Religion? Immigration? There are no "general interest" groups. Everyone tries everything they can think of to get what they want from government (preferably more than the next guy gets), and they don't care about anyone else when they do it.

Get rid of special interest. Geesh.

Another popular technique among politicians is to make implied promises by delivering them as statements of the obvious, but without a proposed solution attached:

"We need more jobs!" Of course we do, but the President doesn't create jobs, unless s/he's adding Cabinet positions or opening new departments— but that's not going to help the average American, because all those jobs will be filled by Friends of the New President. Business creates jobs.

---

9 Here's an idea: why don't we ALL cop to the fact that we have No Fucking Idea how to educate our kids in a world where technology moves so fast that an 11-year-old girl, sitting in a classroom typing 80-words-per-minute with her left thumb— without looking— on a cell phone model you've never even heard of, can text "I just saw Mr. Fenton's ass-crack", while the aforementioned Mr. Fenton is writing on the board WITH FUCKING CHALK, and before he is finished with his totally irrelevant Chaucer quotation, the news of his trouser cleavage, with pictures, is already on the screen of every mobile phone in the school district.

10 Seventy-five years ago, scientists were warning us of a coming Ice Age, as a result of air pollution. Apparently some politicians swore they would do something about it and kept their promise for once, resulting in warnings of a coming Conflagration.

"We've got to end our dependence on foreign oil!" No shit. But somehow we are supposed to do it without drilling, nuclear power, erecting anything in My Backyard, creating pollution or allowing any businesspeople to make money in the process. Good luck.[11, 12]

"We need to make America safe from terrorism!" Know why they're called "Terrorists" and not "Soldiers"? Because they don't wear uniforms, march in columns, or behave in any other way that makes them identifiable as an enemy army. We don't know who they are or where they are hiding. We are powerless to do anything about it. There couldn't be a more-impotent promise that a politician could make than this.[13, 14, 15]

The other most-popular method is to define what your opponent is against (or for), implying that your position is the opposite, without saying so. Later, you can back out of the position by showing that, technically, you never said you were for/against it.

VOTE FOR ME. I'M HALLUCINATORY.

Anyone who thinks he knows how to run the Free World is unqualified for the simple reason that he has obviously underestimated the size and complexity of the problem— and grossly overestimated his abilities. Only a person with profound hubris would run for President. As evidence, I submit a list of our Presidents.

Yet, we gotta have one.

Because we have no choice but to elect a Human Being (with all the negatives entailed therewith), I wish that just once, a candidate would be candid[16] with us. Here's what I'm waiting to hear:

---

11 Interestingly, Mr. Obama is in favor of more offshore drilling. Which party is he in?

12 Oops! Massive oil spill in the Gulf of Mexico— Obama is against drilling again.

13 "I will rid America of termites." That could be a candidate.

14 Nevertheless, Obama has promised this one, too (the terrorism— not the termites.).

15 He got Osama bin Laden. That was a neat trick.

16 Interesting. "Candidate" contains the word "candid", yet they rarely are.

My fellow Americans…

…The United States of America is possibly the most complex object ever created by humankind— and not by design, either. No one knows how it came to be this way, and I cannot, in good conscience, stand here and tell you I have the faintest idea how to run the thing. Consequently, I'm going to have to be brutally honest with you, and what I'm about to say may be deeply disturbing. Is everyone in America sitting down? OK, here goes:

No one is actually "in charge" of the country or ever will be. This is because it is made of countless parts, and, in fact, we have lost track of how many parts there are. We estimate, for example, that there are 78,217,463 Americans and 13,567,601 illegal aliens now on the Federal payroll whom we cannot identify, who work for departments that we cannot locate, or whose activities are a complete mystery. This trend is repeated at every level of government, which brings us to the next subject.

Sometime in late 1974, as a delayed side effect of Lyndon Johnson's attempt to build the Great Society, the number of governmental entities and departments reached Infinity. The GSA has just released the twenty-volume Federal Contact Directory A through B, and expects the entire set to be completed in approximately $4,000^{17}$ years. Once the paper edition is completed, we plan to start working on the Palm Pilot release.

Add to that the number of entities in the Private Sector (currently estimated at $[2x\infty/\pi]^*\Omega$, or roughly 12 x infinity), and you've got yourself a real humdinger of an operation to run. This tangled mess of bureaucracy and self-interest would be difficult enough to manage if I had authority over any of it, but in fact, I don't.

To top it off, it wouldn't matter if I had authority anyway, because of the various ways these countless entities interact and cooperate, which I will now outline for you:

a) Not at all.

The majority of the components of American society are entities that are technically independent of any level of government, although, I am proud to say, not immune from meddling interference. By and large, they are run by people who are motivated by a personal agenda and aren't particularly competent— even to serve their own interests. These components do not effectively communicate, cooperate in any productive manner, or have the same goals. Nevertheless, almost every product, service, innovation, solution, or anything tangible whatsoever is produced by these groups. As President, I have no authority over them unless I want to commandeer them during a war or national emergency— which I would do at my own peril, although Hugo Chavez is getting away with it like a real champ.

b) Barely.

These parts are typically under the aegis of some broad group description, such as the Military/Industrial Complex, Education, Labor, Hypen-Americans, Baby-boomers, Golden-agers, Illegal Aliens, NAMBLA, Pro-whateverers and other clever names. Various alliances among these groups will spring forth around election time if they perceive a common cause. These alliances, however, will evaporate at a moment's notice if any group thinks of a way to get a bigger share of whatever pie they are struggling to divide. They will then turn on one other like rabid dingoes. As President, I have no authority over them, but I can get them to cooperate with me occasionally by lying to them.

c) Only under duress.

The States comprise the majority of this group. Once a bunch of States tried to start their own gig. A huge fight erupted and it was extremely bloody and expensive for everyone involved. It was known as the Civil War. Some of you older folks may have learned about it in school. Nevertheless, no states have tried it again, but plenty of people are still very touchy about the whole affair. Ever since, these entities have worked together only begrudgingly, and occasionally a fight breaks out over flag-flying or the content of bronze plaques. As President, I have no authority whatsoever over these groups.

d) Marginally.

The Legislative and Judiciary branches of Government are examples of this type. Once in a while, these groups will gather in the House Chamber and pretend to listen to me for an hour or so. Immediately afterward, ranking members of the opposition party will appear on television to say 'Liar, Liar, Pants on Fire', 'Boom-shakalaka' or 'Hey, Nonny Nonny'. Occasionally, I will suggest Legislation (known as Presidential Initiatives) to these folks and they will have a good laugh at my expense. As President, I have no authority over these groups except the Veto, which is my way of delaying legislation long enough for my private-sector friends to dump appropriate stocks, invest in firms that are about to receive huge federal contracts or get out of the country.

The few allies that I used to have when I was a Senator are still angry about the lies I told about them during the last primary campaign. They, too, will still pretend to like me when I enter the Chamber for the State of the Union Address.

e) Somewhat sloppily.

These groups consist of people under my direct control, such as my Cabinet, political advisers and staff. Most of these will pretend to obey me, and they will occasionally do some nice scurrying when I bark out orders in a crisis. The truth is, as President, I have very little authority over them unless I am horny or want something to eat in the middle of the night. I can, however, get a Starbucks cart put in the West Wing if I want to— and I just might.

As you can clearly see, if I stand here and tell you all the things I'm going to do as President, I am obviously full of shit. The United States— not to mention the Free World— is like a vast, lumbering ship with three hundred and eight-million steering wheels. Assuming we somehow agreed to do so, we could all Heave Hard to Starboard at precisely the same moment and it will be a very, very long time before anyone notices any change in direction.

So here's what I propose: I'll stop telling you I have all the answers if you will all accept the idea that YOU— as citizens— are in charge of your own lives, for the most part. We'll send cops and firefighters when appropriate, keep the water running, the lights on and the garbage mostly picked up— but other than that you're going to have to do most of the heavy lifting to affect your own fate.

Keep in mind that when all hell breaks loose, like a war or natural disaster, all I'm empowered to do as President is to send various types of government employees to the scene, so it should be no surprise to anyone that these situations quickly turn to puppy-shit.

As your President, I will pledge to do the following for America:

- Try not to lose the keys to the place;
- Resist the temptation to flip every switch— especially the unlabeled ones;
- Stop drinking the milk directly from the carton, metaphorically speaking;
- Take out the garbage without having to be nagged;
- Call if I'm going to be late.

So that's it. I won't screw with you, but you have to wipe your own noses. Elect me and I will do everything in my astonishingly limited power to return your country in recognizable condition at the end of my term(s).

Good night, and God(s) [or not] Bless America.

IT'S THE PRESIDENT OF THE UNITED STATES— NOT YOUR MOMMY.

My fellow Americans…

…I am speaking with you today to announce the formation of a new department within the Federal Government— a department that has been created because of the tremendous feedback from you— the citizens of these Great United States. As I promised during my campaign, I was going to be the President who LISTENED to the People. You have spoken, and today we are taking bold action.

If I may quote from the Preamble to the Constitution V 4.5.1 beta, available for download at: *www.myGOV/myUS/myLAWS/ myRIGHTS/whatsinitforme?/gimmegimmegimme.html/preamble*:

"We the People of the United States, in Order to form a more Perfect Illusion, Ensure that every Citizen feels good about her/himself, Establish equal outcomes, Promote everyone beyond his abilities, and make everyone feel Secure even at the expense of our Posterity, do ordain and establish this Constitution for the United States of America, while recognizing that we are despicable people who deserve to be hated by the rest of the World— particularly the French."

As leader of a country that is dedicated to making sure none of you is ever inconvenienced by events caused by reality or other uncontrollable forces, and in the wake of the terrorist attacks on 9/11, several natural disasters of unprecedented scale, and a spate of incidents involving people with bombs in their underpants, I am humbled to report that those of us in every level of government have received nearly countless complaints about our inability to predict, foresee, divine, forestall, prevent, mitigate, and/or rectify these events. Hundreds of thousands of Americans have been affected with unimaginable suffering— ranging from instant gruesome death all the way to loss of self-esteem.

Americans are demanding to know why we didn't predict these events, and until now, government officials have given them the same, lame, unacceptable explanation:

We didn't predict these disasters because they were— frankly— unimaginable.

Well, that's not good enough anymore. Just because no one in their wildest dreams imagined that a bunch of Islamic Fundamentalists would move to the United States, shave their beards, pretend for years to be assimilating into our culture by adopting Western attire, swilling beer and hanging out in titty bars, while taking flying lessons (but not landing lessons) so they could hijack four commercial jets on the same day and crash them into our major landmarks, bringing them down in a fiery conflagration the likes of which have been unseen since the bombing of Dresden— *No!* Just because no one could possibly have imagined events like these is no excuse.

That's why today I am announcing the creation of the *Department of Predicting the Unimaginable.* We have located the nation's best psychics, seers, tea-leaf twiddlers, palmists, conspiracy theorists, crackpots and wackos and brought them together to form this new department. I am also proud to announce that this will not cost the American taxpayers one dime, because every one of these talented individuals was already employed at some level of government. Moreover, their departures from their present positions will have no ill effects on government operations because they weren't doing anything anyway.

This new department— chaired by that hot chick on Ghost Whisperer— in conjunction with its various sub departments;

- The Office of Locating Someone to Blame;

- The Finger-Pointing Commission;

- The Division of I Saw the Whole Thing Coming, and its sister entity—

- The I Tried To Tell Them But No One Would Listen Committee;

- The President's Panel of 20/20 Hindsight;

- The Congressional Library of Incriminating Documents; and

- The Manager of Pre-Sacked Department Heads,

... will take on the crucial task of making certain that never again will anything bad happen to Americans— however farfetched.

For the convenience of our citizens, satellite offices will be located in Cassadega, Florida; Lily Dale, New York; Boulder, Colorado; Roswell, New Mexico; Ann Arbor, Michigan; Sedona, Arizona; Eureka Springs, Arkansas; Burlington, Vermont; and all convenience stores, gas stations, organic co-ops, Trader Joe's, Hummer dealerships and cosmetic surgery clinics in California.[17] In the event of a nationwide power failure, terrorist attack, dirty bomb detonation or Harmonic Convergence, our Emergency Operations Command Ship, the USS Enigma, will be permanently stationed somewhere in the Bermuda Triangle (we think).

Ladies and gentlemen, the government's job is to hold the clammy little hand of every frightened person in America, and this administration takes that responsibility very seriously. Today we are taking bold action.

In closing, I would like to recall the words of the immortal John "F-Dogg" Kennedy:

'Ask not what your Country can do for you;
Get in your Country's damn face about it.'

Thank you, and good night.

---

17 The California Regional Office is located in Bolinas, but no employees have yet been able to report to work, because no one can find the town.

I'M THE PRESIDENT. FAR OUT.

We have now reached a point in history where all Presidential candidates are more likely to have used drugs than not— with many admitting (bragging?) publicly that they have done so. This trend lends credence to the long-standing assertion that drug use leads to a life of crime.

It also makes one wonder about our country's drug policies. It is now possible for a young person to smoke a little bud and, if caught by the authorities, face a life of ruin, despair, and corn-holing by violent criminals in prison, or, if not apprehended— become the President of the United States.

This new Chief Executive, as with all the competing candidates, will undoubtedly have employed a campaign antidrug stance to get elected. Anyone who cannot see the deep irony in this may now be excused from class for the rest of the semester.

A QUESTION THAT HAS BEEN BUGGING ME FOR A LONG TIME, AND WHICH HAS BECOME EVER MORE RELEVANT AS OF THE 2008 ELECTION, FOLLOWED UP BY SOME FOLLOW-UP QUESTIONS.

If a person who is 1/2 ethnic is considered "ethnic," then why is a person who is 1/2 white also considered "ethnic"?

Is it racist to ask that question?

Why isn't Obama just another White Guy in the White House?

How small does the percentage of "ethnicity" need to get before someone is considered "white"?

Is anyone "white"?

Thank you.

SUGGESTED AMENDMENTS TO THE
FIRST AMENDMENT

I like the First Amendment as much as the next guy or gal, but I think it has caused us a bit of trouble over the years— especially of late. It is, of course, one of the Cornerstones of American Freedom That We All Hold Dear, but because Americans are incapable of exercising a right without abusing the hell out of it, I would like to suggest some modest conditions that we might apply— just for the sake of civility, you understand. To wit:

CONGRESS SHALL MAKE NO LAW RESPECTING AN ESTABLISHMENT OF RELIGION, OR PROHIBITING THE FREE EXERCISE THEREOF;

- Unless the religion involves a bunch of self-righteous, glassy-eyed drones who feel compelled to periodically burst into the public sphere with the intention of infecting the populace like zombies in some B-horror flick;

- Unless its clergy has a penchant for little boys, little girls, peep shows, pornography, methamphetamine, anonymous homosexual encounters, leather Nazi garb, etc.;

- Unless tithe funds are used to build a theme park;

- Unless it involves Christian Rock Music— an affront to both Christianity and Rock Music;

- Unless a JumboTron and/or front-of-house sound engineer is necessary to conduct services;

- Unless the religion endorses the subordination of women, gays or other groups of people created by the same God they purport to worship.

- Unless the religion can in any way justify harming another person because of that person's differing religious beliefs or lack thereof.

...OR ABRIDGING THE FREEDOM OF SPEECH,

- Unless the speaker is clearly an idiot, nimrod, oaf, doofus, schmuck, dimwit, dickhead, shit-for-brains, etc.;
- Unless the speaker has already said the same thing three times to the same listener(s) in the course of one conversation;
- Unless the speaker is drunk (see #2, above);
- Unless the speaker has already said the thing once on Larry King, CNN, Letterman, Oprah, Bill Maher, etc.;
- Unless the speaker is Jesse Jackson, Pat Buchanan, Ann Coulter, Arianna Huffington or anyone else whose name appears on a list that I will periodically update; — Oops, I almost forgot Alec Baldwin;
- Unless you are Michael Moore;
- Unless the speaker is any other celebrity who is under the mistaken impression that we give a shit what s/he thinks;
- Unless the speaker insists on explaining a sophomoric, oversimplified, misinformed version of an obsolete, flawed, or well-discredited position such as holocaust denial, phrenology, homeopathy, communism, astrology, etc.;
- Unless the speaker is a political analyst stating anything after-the-fact to support a previous wild guess that somehow turned out to be correct;
- Unless that fucking picture of Che Guevera (you know the one) is used in any publications, apparel, posters, videos, or any other media having to do with said speech;
- As long as you keep your voice down.

...OR OF THE PRESS;

- Unless there are already too many media outlets espousing the same position. For example, if we have the New York Times, do we really need the Washington Post? If we have Fox News, do we need any other conservative media whatsoever?
- Unless the media outlet is owned by Rupert Murdock;
- Unless you are a journalist who makes up shit;
- Unless you are an ill-informed, ranting blogger with abominable research skills, horrible spelling and grammar and a myopic world view, who feels compelled to use profanity and other lazy shit instead of carefully crafting a position;
- Unless you are a self-appointed social critic who would never have his book published in the traditional channels owing to their competence at preventing such drivel from entering the information stream.

...OR THE RIGHT OF THE PEOPLE PEACEABLY TO ASSEMBLE,

- Unless it's an obviously pointless exercise such as a Peace March, Million-Whatever March, or Citizen's Against Today's Big Issue March which has *clearly* and *repeatedly* proved to have *no* effect on Government policy at *any* level, but creates significant hardship for ordinary citizens who are trying to get to fucking Starbucks;
- Unless 51% or more of the women in the demonstration have Euro-Pits;
- Unless Al Sharpton is involved in any manner;
- Same for Louis Farrakhan;
- And Jerry Falwell or that Promise-Keeper guy;
- Cindy Sheehan (Oy, gevalt!);
- Actually, I hate demonstrations— who am I kidding? They should be outlawed altogether.

…and to petition the Government for a redress of grievances.

- Unless your grievance is rooted in the fact that you are bull-headed, intentionally uneducated, high, narcissistic, sadistic, self-hating, lazy, conniving, greedy, self-righteous, ignorant, or you have already had plenty of grievance-redressing floor time and should shut-the-fuck-up and let somebody else complain for once;

- Unless you are not a citizen, don't vote, or don't pay taxes;

- Unless you rape, rob, fleece, flim-flam, degrade, humiliate, imprison, maim, or kill other human beings (OK, pets, too);

- Unless you haven't redressed the grievances against yourself by people in your own life such as your spouse, kids, cowork-ers, employees, servants, constituents, prisoners, slaves, door-man, maid, store clerks, wait staff, sanitation workers, etc.

That wasn't too bad, now was it? For the typical decent person, these conditions should be fairly easy to meet without a significant change in lifestyle. Only the selfish, whining, larcenous, meddling, pushy, pedantic, overbearing jagoffs will have their "rights" compromised— and frankly, who gives a shit? These people are ALWAYS exercising their rights— right up our patooties. Raise your hand if you're tired of it!

WE INTERRUPT OUR
REGULARLY-SCHEDULED BOOK FOR THIS

SPECIAL PRESENTATION

CONSISTING PRIMARILY OF THE SAME SORT OF DRIVEL
WITH SLIGHTLY DIFFERENT TYPOGRAPHY, MORE CHARTS
AND NO NARRATIVE THREAD.
A BUNCH OF RANDOM JUNK, REALLY, BUT USEFUL
FOR MAKING THE BOOK THICKER, WHICH CONFERS HIGHER
MORAL AUTHORITY THAN SOME ANEMIC LITTLE PAMPHLET,
ALTHOUGH PAMPHLETS WERE GOOD ENOUGH
FOR THOMAS PAINE.

BUT THAT WAS THE 1700's.

AND IT WAS THOMAS PAINE.

MORAL-DILEMMA EXERCISES

Sometimes, people discover their true beliefs only when faced with a difficult decision— a situation that presents a problem for those of us who live in a society that insulates us from pain, need, ambiguity and other forms of discomfort. In our society we routinely expect others to make those hard decisions for us, and we blame everything bad that happens on someone else. In a system such as this, it can be easy to become numbed to your true feelings about anything— unlike those who lived through The Great Depression or World War II, for example, who often possess a certain, enviable, clarity.

Below are two scenarios that you can use to help identify your true political stripe. By considering these hypothetical situations, you may learn more about your inner "feelings," which might have been suppressed through theocratic indoctrination, excess fatty foods, sex addiction, or higher education. Warning: it is possible that you may discover some "inconvenient truths" about yourself— like, "Wow, am I a hypocrite!" or "By golly, I am full of shit!"

Proceed carefully and keep in mind that there are no right answers— only Right and Left answers.

Exercise 1:

You are a Progressive Liberal with a hundred bucks to spend on a Cause: in this case, Helping The Hungry. How can your $100 be put to the highest and best use? Here are your choices:

- Donate the money to a homeless shelter in your city run by a religious group, whose staff will try to indoctrinate the clients despite the fact that those clients are incurable alcoholics, drug addicts, schizophrenics, etc. This charity can deliver seventy cents' worth of food for every dollar you donate. The other thirty cents ends up in the coffers of a church that you, an atheist, do not support. Although all the clients at this facility are Authentic Victims for one reason or another, they are also Americans: citizens of a country you despise because of its long history of colonialism, hegemony and cultural genocide.

- Donate the money to a secular NGO that employs idealistic young college students in an effort to distribute food to Muslim fundamentalists in northwestern Africa— people who practice polygamy, institutionally subjugate women and engage in forced female genital mutilation. Support of this NGO will allow you to use the term "Timbouctu" in casual conversation. This organization can deliver ten cents' worth of food for every dollar you donate. The rest goes to meager salaries for the idealistic young people, overhead, fuel, marketing, and payments to corrupt African warlords who commit atrocities against their own people. The plight of these Africans had been adopted as a pet subject by a prominent journalist at the New York Times— prior to its bankruptcy.

- Attend a Hunger Awareness benefit sponsored by a well-known think tank. This event will feature a keynote address by a rock star, and will be attended by numerous good-looking celebrities, prominent politicians, and noted intellectuals— any of whom with which you might get a photo taken. No food will be distributed to anyone other than the party attendees, but there will be monster press coverage, which means that Hunger Awareness will be very high after the event, attracting many more caring people to the cause who can be tasked with the actual work of feeding some poor schmucks. A hundred Bucks will not get you a great table and you have nothing to wear. Cash bar.

Exercise 2:

You are a Born-Again Christian man who found religion after spending your early adult years as a meth addict, living in a filthy flop-house with no running water. You acquired money for drugs through shoplifting, petty scams and pimping your crack-whore girlfriend. Although she died of AIDS, and you had anonymous sex with possibly scores (you can't remember) of male and female partners, you somehow remained uninfected— which you now attribute to Divine Intervention.

You have since cleaned up your life, accepted Jesus Christ as your personal savior, are now married and have a daughter who is a freshman at a public high school. You have received a phone call from the school Principal requesting a meeting with her and a mincing guidance counselor. At this meeting you learn that your daughter is involved in a contest with two other girls to see who can administer oral sex to the most members of the Varsity basketball squad. At the time of the intervention, your daughter has a solid B+ scholastic average, and is the clear frontrunner (frontkneeler, more accurately) in the contest. How should you handle the situation?

- Use the incident to start a movement to restore prayer to the public school system.

- Exhibit shock, anger, revulsion and disappointment that your daughter would be involved in such disgusting activity, causing her intense guilt and self-hatred for failing to follow your shining example as parents— emotionally scarring her for life and starting her on an unending series of inappropriate relationships with abusive men, ultimately resulting in your shock at finding her starring in a porn video you downloaded from the internet.

- Employ stories of your own sordid sexual history to find common ground, demonstrate forgiveness, show your own vulnerability, and strengthen the family bonds through shared adversity. This will necessarily involve revealing your disgusting past to your unknowing wife.

- Get your wife to handle it and throw up an impenetrable wall of silence between you and your daughter that will remain unresolved upon your death.

- Explain that her behavior has brought shame to the entire family. Force her to give up her friends and put her in parochial school with heavy emphasis on Bible study.

- Refuse to believe any of it, upbraid the school administration for slandering your "good girl" and file a lawsuit.

- Upbraid the administration for stopping the contest when your daughter had a clear chance of winning. Demand that she be declared the winner despite the premature end of the contest.

- Determine how the contest has affected the team standings before responding.

STICK AND STONES, PART TWO.

One aspect of PC that completely baffles the typical Middle is the idea that offensive speech is essentially equivalent to physical violence. Utilizing a $1.2 million Rebuild America grant from my new buddy in the White House, I instructed my Department of Self-Serving Research to look into this matter.

The study produced some interesting results, despite 79% attrition of grant funds through the bookkeeping category "Administrative Overhead-Other."

Our research revealed several important differences between the effects of offensive speech and physical violence. A representative study sample is shown below:

Plate One (following page)shows a study participant after the application of offensive speech. The participant was subjected to interpersonal communication consisting of:

- Racial slurs;
- Cultural stereotyping;
- Bad words;
- Accurate, yet uncomfortable, observations by others of his physical, psychological and behavior traits;
- Disagreement with his viewpoints;
- Correction of factual errors in his expressed opinions;
- Direct verbal interaction with white males;
- Howling laughter, huffing, hooting, snorting, spluttering and other forms of derision;
- Vitriol;
- Eye-rolling, deep sighs with accompanying slumping posture, knee slapping and other negative nonverbal communication.

After the session, the participant was examined by a team of alternative-medicine practitioners, psychologists, sociology professors, ethnic persons and feminists representing an accurate cultural cross-section of Progressive Liberal society.

The panel found that the participant's injuries included:

1. Hurt feelings;
2. Loss of self-esteem;
3. That's pretty much it.

PLATE 1

Plate 2, below, shows the same participant after the application of a righteous beat-down. After this session, the participant was examined by the triage team at the local teaching hospital.

The participant's injuries now include:

1. Cerebral hematoma;
2. Brain swelling;
3. Concussion;
4. Fractured jawbone;
5. Detached retina;
6. Permanent vision loss in left eye;
7. Loss of teeth;
8. Crushed hyoid bone;
9. Tinnitus;
10. Hurt feelings;
11. Loss of self-esteem;
12. Loss of feeling in right arm.

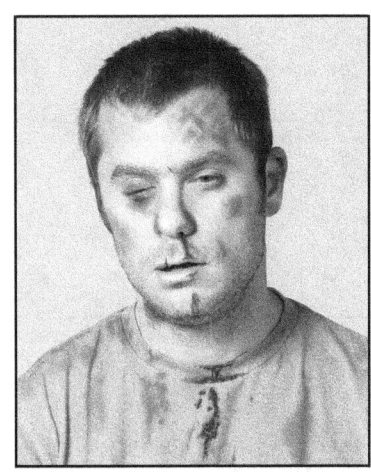

PLATE 2

DISTRIBUTION OF FREEDOM OF SPEECH
IN AMERICAN SOCIETY

Despite all the rhetoric to the contrary, all members of our society do not equally share free speech. Some groups of Americans can say anything they want about other Americans and never need to apologize. Any group that can achieve Victim Status gains the right to say anything about its Perpetrator without regard to truth, fairness, decorum or any other restraint.

Listed below are words, phrases, concepts, observations, stereotypes & behaviors[1] whose use will get you fired, forced to resign, made to publicly apologize, and/or prevent your vanity-published book from being picked up by a major publisher if you are a member of Ethnic Group 1: GreedyWhiteMales:

BANNED WORDS LIST:

"_____"

"_____"

"_____"

"_____ _____"

"____ ____ _____"

"___"

"_____ __ _____ ___"

"_____"

"_____ _____ _____"

"_____"

"_____ ___"

etc...

_____

1 The actual words, phrases, concepts, etc. have been intentionally omitted because as a GreedyWhiteMale, I'm not allowed to use them in ANY context— including a treatise on the idea that I'm not allowed to use them. Besides, it's the *relative quantities* of banned stuff that matters.

Listed below are words, phrases, concepts, observations, stereotypes & behaviors whose use will get you fired, forced to resign, made to publicly apologize, and/or prevent your vanity-published book from being picked up by a major publisher if you are a female, gay and/or a member of Ethnic Groups 2,3,4,5,6,7,8, etc:

BANNED WORDS LIST:

Note the slight disparity in the size of these lists. In addition to the Gender/Ethnicity Variable, the physical location, political environment and other factors where the speech takes place influences the Speech Freedom Index as well, as shown on the following page:

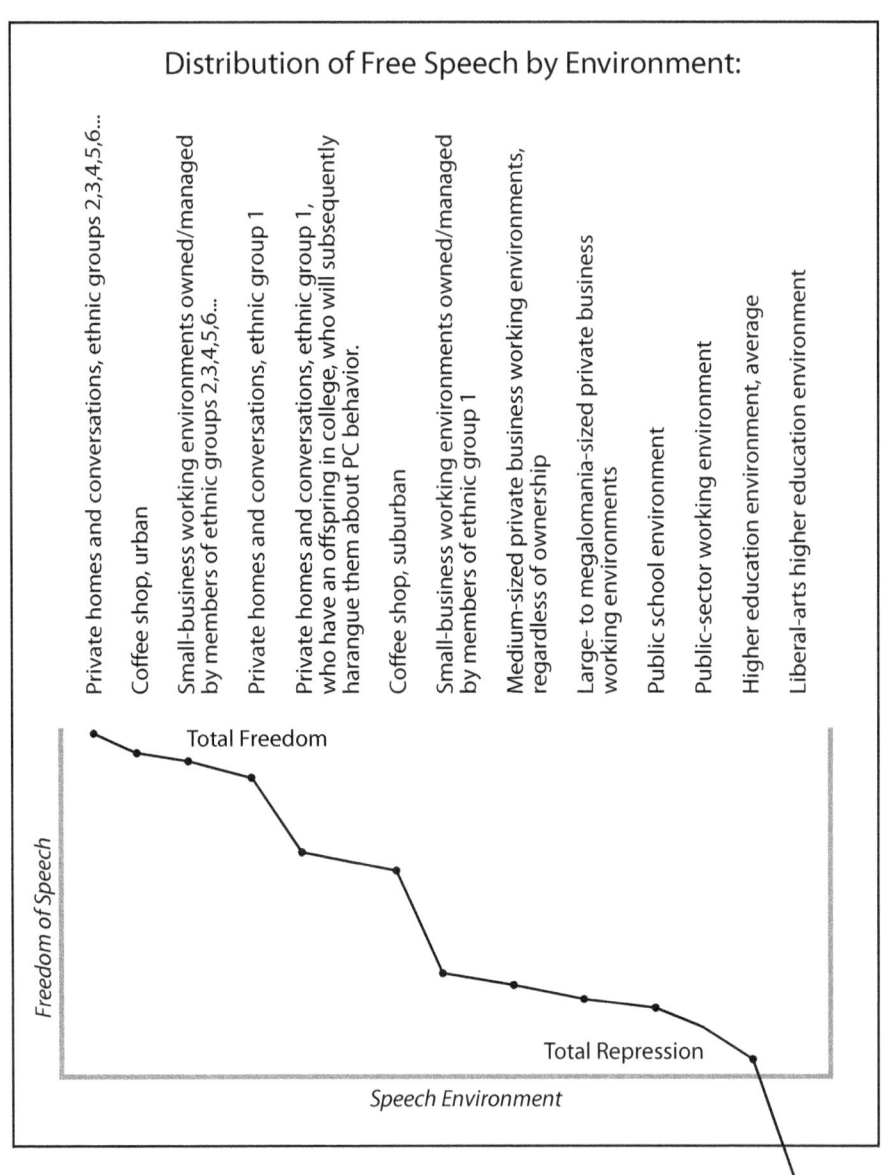

Distribution of Free Speech by Environment:

By studying the chart, we can see that there is a wide disparity of restriction on free speech in our society, ranging from complete freedom for certain groups in private situations to the most severe restrictions in— of all places— our institutions of higher learning, also known as the repositories and protectorates of intellectual freedom.

Let us explore some of the implications of this data:

- The future leaders of one of the longest-lived free societies in history are being trained in the most speech-repressive environments in our society.

- Some groups are allowed (almost encouraged) to practice hate speech, while others are not, resulting in yet another societal double standard, created— ironically— by a group that avows to hate societal double standards.

- Congressional debates are nowhere near as interesting as they were, say, 150 years ago.

- It is becoming exceedingly difficult to form a good, snappy comeback without the availability of offensive derogatory terminology.

SPECIAL SECTION JUST FOR RIGHT-WINGERS

I really shouldn't be revealing this, but it's just TOO GOOD. I'm going to describe a surefire way to irritate the bejeezes out of Lefties. It's called a Bell Curve and it's easy to grasp, simple to deploy, and works every time! Turn the page[2] for complete instructions:

---

2 Greenies: most of this page, and the entire opposite one is blank because I couldn't figure out how to get the charts to fit without uncomfortable typesetting compromises. If this book becomes a bestseller, this is going to result in an appalling waste of paper. Outrage emails may be directed to: paperwaste@mindyourownvote.com.

Here's how the Leftie Bell Curve Pimpslap Device works:

Every human trait is expressed to a different degree depending on the individual. Take height, for example. Some people have more of it (tall people), most have some of it (average) and a few have less (short). If we plot the height of a given number of people chosen at random, the chart will look like this:

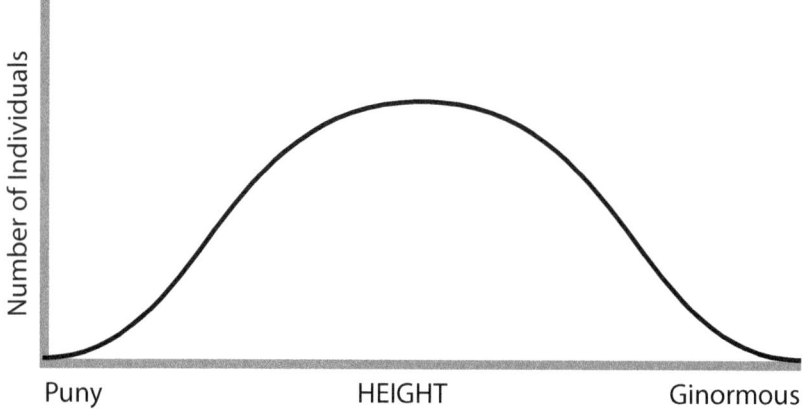

If we double, triple, or quazoople the number of people— still chosen at random— the chart will still look like this:

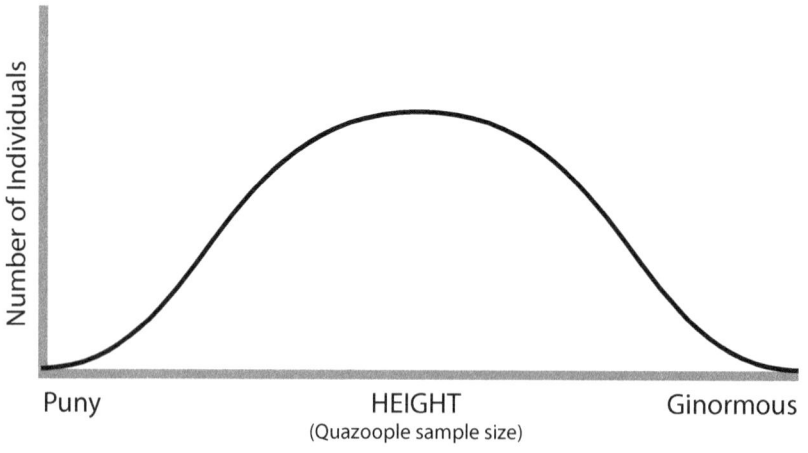

Reading from left to right, the chart shows that a few people are short, most of 'em are average, and a few are tall. This distribution curve works for plotting nearly every type of human physical, mental and behavioral attribute. This drives liberals completely batshit, because it conflicts with one of their cherished ideals— that we should pretend to be unaware of differences among individuals, groups or cultures. (Somehow, we are supposed to Celebrate Diversity at the same time [see "Cognitive Dissonance"]).

The trouble is that the damn curve represents a continuum— which happens to be the vehicle to which we are all clinging in this thrilling ride of life, and however much it bugs some people to admit it— we are not all the same. Not even twins are exactly the same (many, however, are close enough for a good sexual fantasy. But I digress.).

Let's explore some useful knowledge we can glean about various subjects by using the Bell Curve:

Plotted below are the results of all the reform movements ever saddled upon the pathetic human species. The horizontal (or "X" axis, in Chartese) plots the level of success of the reform movements depicted in the chart. The extreme left side of the axis represents "Complete Failure," while the extreme right shows "Spectacular Success" (there is no correlation whatsoever with "Right" and "Left" in the political sense, so don't get excited, Teabaggers.)

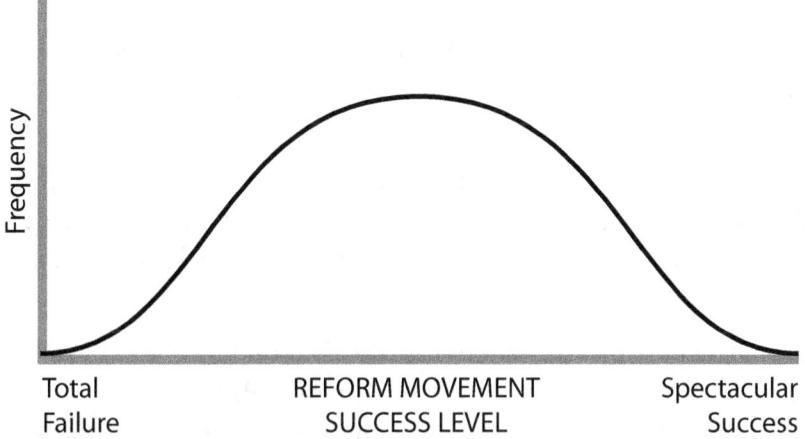

| Total | REFORM MOVEMENT | Spectacular |
| Failure | SUCCESS LEVEL | Success |

As the chart clearly illustrates, a few reform movements resulted in Complete Failure (the Inquisition and French Revolution come to mind), while most were partially successful, and a few were Spectacular Successes (I can't think of any examples, but trust me, the Bell Curve never lies.).

Next, we shall graph the data in another illuminating way. In this case, the X-axis represents which features of the reform movements were actually implemented in the course of their typical partially successful deployment. On the left, the worst features of the given reform movement, and on the right the best features (again, no political correlation).

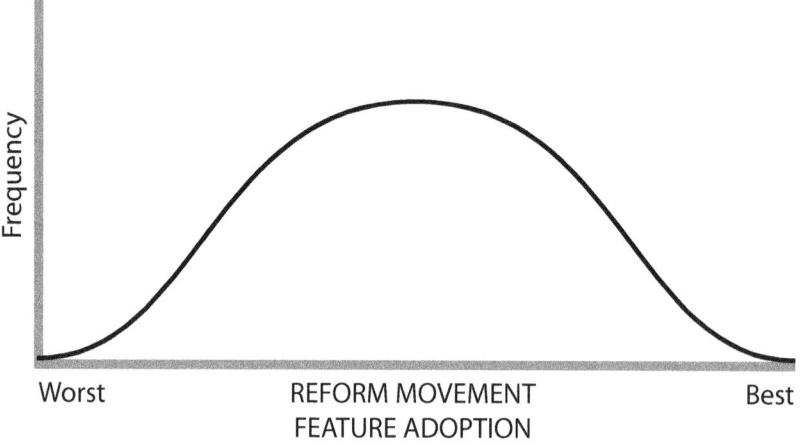

What is revealed in this plot is why everything is generally mediocre: The best and worst features of Reform are rarely adopted, but the average, middling parts all-too-often are.

The bell curve works with any type of data that depicts anything about people— and, well, almost any aspect of anything. To defeat the Mighty Bell Curve, you have to engage in some impressive mental gymnastics. Below are two examples.

The next chart illustrates how the RWEs (you guys) see things. In this view, Perfect Piety is on the right, and Piety Paucity is on the left. (In this case there is a loose political correlation on the X-axis— at least in your opinion.)

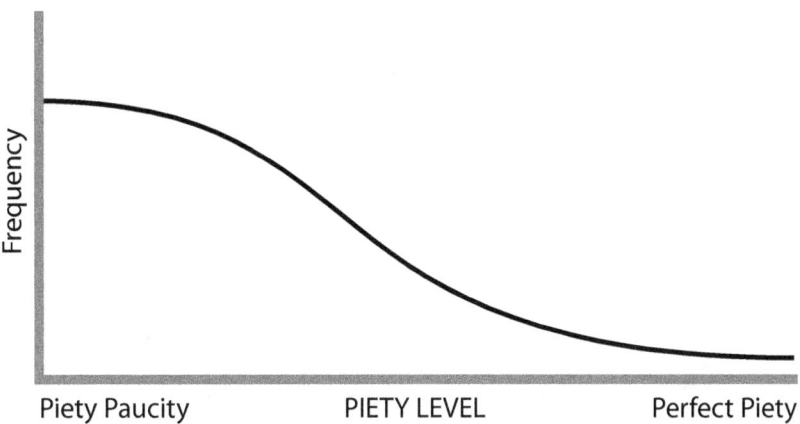

Piety Paucity   PIETY LEVEL   Perfect Piety

As the graph illustrates, very few achieve piety; most people don't even seem to be trying; and a whole bunch are lolling around in moral filth (happily, it seems— but that's another subject.) This, however, does not explain why there are so many people who still believe they are behaving piously. The self-delusion graph, shown below, explains how this phenomenon occurs:

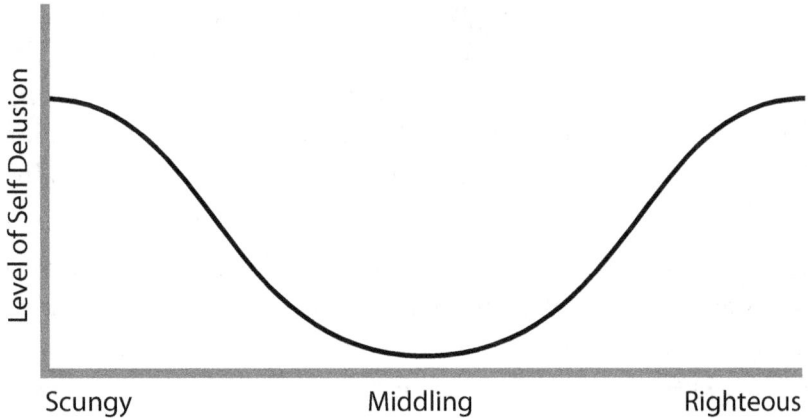

Scungy   Middling   Righteous

This graph displays a negative bell curve in which those represented by the end points are highly self-delusional, and those in the middle have accepted themselves as the moderately pathetic shlubs they are.

If we overlay these two groups of data, we see that the people represented on the left are debauched but don't know it; those in the middle are to varying degrees aware and accepting of their middling character; and those on the right are in denial of their shortcomings and consider themselves morally superior.

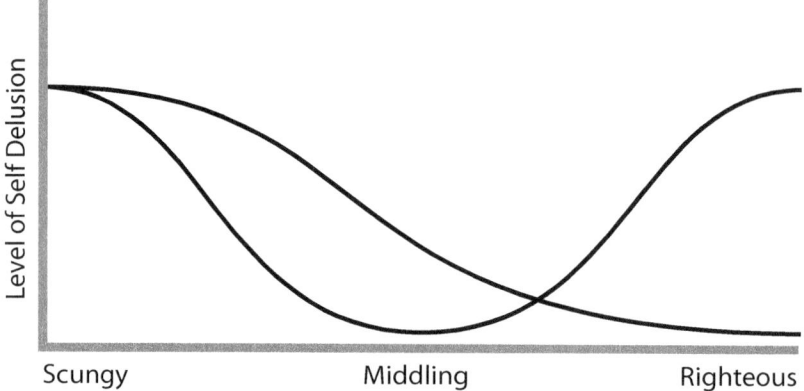

It also shows why you folks believe that anyone can be saved, no matter how pathetic. Accordingly, your reform efforts are applied to everyone, ceaselessly. The problem is this: some people (and they're all over the chart, with a whole bunch in the Middle) are simply irredeemable, and will never meet your standards. They won't stop doing things that they enjoy, just because *you* consider them sinful. Spanking The Monkey comes to mind, as an example. Good luck stopping that.

Next, we will examine the LWE world view. The X-axis of this chart represents all human traits. On the left is The Left, and on the right, The Right (in this case there is a ironclad correlation with Political Left and Right). Everyone else is somewhere in the middle (this includes all members of the Third World, regardless of political leaning). The Y-axis (vertical) represents Reform Potential and its midpoint is the Reproach/Contempt boundary. For clarity, a line is struck across the chart at this level.

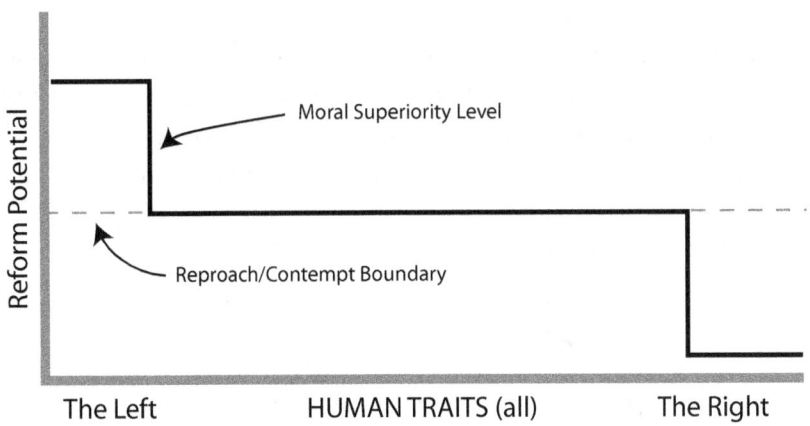

As the data shows, those on the Left are above reproach, so no reform is necessary. Most of humanity lies precisely on the boundary and, as such, are fair subjects for reform effort. Those on the Right, who are beneath contempt, are simply irredeemable and not worth the wasting of resources (most Red-state Idiots are on this part of the chart). Because the LWE refuses to employ the Bell Curve, he mistakenly believes that there is a bottomless fount of Reform Potential awaiting his attention— which he slathers mercilessly on the Middle.

Note, also, that the LWE chart is more complex than the others— particularly the RWE chart. This is because the LWEs employ the Scientific Method as a tool to obfuscate the fact that their philosophy is in fact a religion— one that is in direct competition with yours.

Only through deliberate, concentrated effort can one hammer the Bell Curve into other interesting and useful shapes— because of that pesky continuum thing. But extremists are very good at this activity, and throughout our history, extremists from both sides have forged the most intriguing and fanciful frameworks, upon which have been erected some of our most-enduring and cherished institutions: human sacrifice, witch trials, debtor's prison, slavery, The Crusades, Political Correctness, Scientology, gay-bashing, and homeopathy to name but a few.

Yet the Bell Curve persists. A recent meta-analysis (the statistical analysis of everyone else's statistics, relieving the researcher from the tedious work of producing new information) of all data of any kind ever produced about human beings, bore the following fruit:

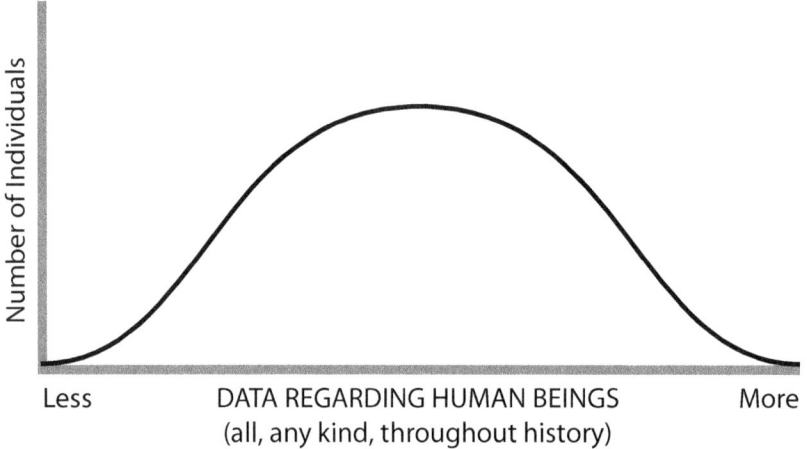

This graph shows the statistical distribution of all human traits: physical, mental, intellectual, metaphysical, metaphorical, moral, perversional, delusional, imaginary and wished-for. As in the previous graphs, if you're on the left, you ain't got none of the trait, and if you're on the right, you're, like, totally ripped. Note the telltale, Evil Bell Curve, suggesting that not everyone is the same. Damn.

One trait, however, defied all the rest of the data. Below is the statistical distribution of this— as it turns out— rare and elusive trait:

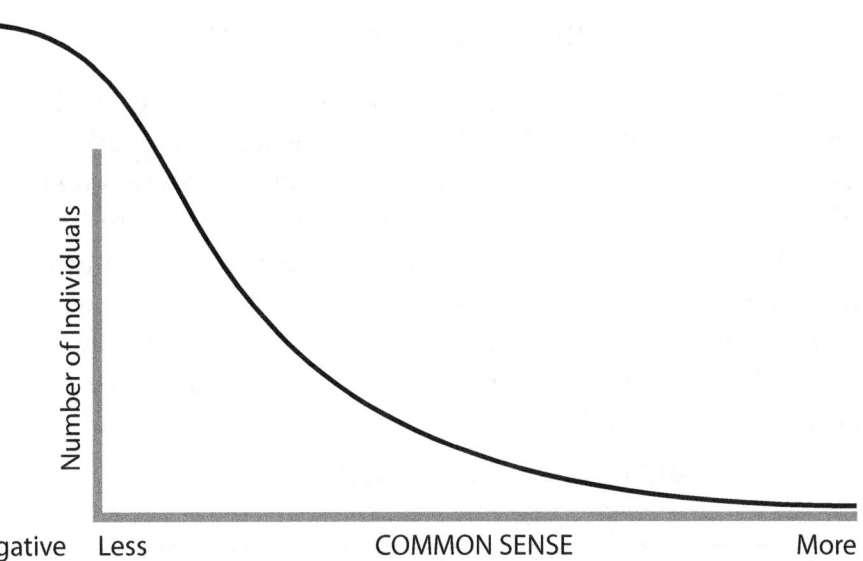

The trait shown in this chart is Common Sense, an unfortunately named item if there ever was one. The meta-analysis revealed that despite its moniker, this trait has been startlingly rare throughout human history, and that the rate of its occurrence has not increased over time, which came as a complete surprise to the researchers for some reason.

Anyway, if you ever find yourself losing an argument with a Leftie, just whip out a Bell Curve and shove it in his face— he'll run for cover faster n' a OWS protester dodgin' a rubber bullet.

AMERICAN RED/BLUE DEATH MATRIX

A handy way to compare/contrast the two groups is to look at their respective attitudes regarding the subject of killing one another. In the matrix below, we can see just how neatly the two groups cleave across the moral divide of Life and Death. An interesting feature that is revealed is that neither group is uniformly for or against killing other people— it depends on the circumstances. These subtle distinctions, however, are the source of a considerable amount of the hatred these two groups hold for each another, and— of course— more suffering for the Middle caught in the middle.

AMERICAN RED/BLUE DEATH MATRIX

ITEM	RED STATER	BLUE STATER
OK To Kill 'Em? Section (When is it morally acceptable to end a human life?)		
Gleam in your father's eye	NO	YES
Zygote	NO	YES
Stem cell	NO	YES
First-trimester fetus	NO	YES
Second-trimester fetus	NO	YES
Third-trimester fetus	NO	NO, but we don't like it.
Baby	Maybe [1]	NO
Teenager	Maybe	NO
Adult	Maybe	NO
Terminally ill adult	NO	YES[2]
Capital-Punishment Section (When is it morally acceptable to fry someone?)		
Death-row inmate, shot wife	Of course!	How can you take a life?
Spree Killer	Slowly & painfully, if possible	NO, probably an incest victim
American military commander ordering the killing of civilians during armed conflict	NO, he was just doing his job to preserve American Freedom	Definitely— he's a murderous demon, just like everyone in the military[3]
Anyone else's military commander ordering the killing of civilians during armed conflict	Absolutely— what he did is barbaric!	No way— we should mind our own business and stop being so imperialistic
For gassing own citizens	YES	NO
Flying plane into skyscraper	YES	Depends[4]

Attitudes and Prejudices Section (When do we care whether someone gets offed?)		
Christian gets hit by bus	Care deeply	Don't give a shit
Muslim, Jew, Hindu, Animist, Shinto, Secular Humanist, Atheist, Wiccan, Rastafarian, etc. gets hit by bus	Don't give a shit— asshole wasn't going to get into Heaven anyway	Care deeply— probably a victim of American Imperialist Hegemony
Americans get blown to bits by suicide bomber in another country	Care deeply— offense against America	Deserved it simply by being an American[5]

Footnotes to Red/Blue Death Matrix

1 In a war, for example— no problem.

2 Requires either a lucid victim or someone who "knows what Doris would have wanted" to authorize pulling tubes.

3 Cops, too.

4 Was skyscraper filled with GreedyCapitalists? In that case, NO.

5 Foreign exchange students, Peace Corps volunteers, hippie backpackers, and Democratic Party embassy personnel excluded. In these cases, although it's deeply tragic, the bomber could only see things from his inherited cultural perspective, and, as such, is not to blame.

The matrix reveals several interesting things:

The Blue Stater column requires significantly more footnotes. These are necessary because Blue Staters employ a conceptual model called Moral Relativism. Basically, it means that questions of morality always "depend." On circumstances. On what Alec Baldwin thinks. On whether the consequences of the moral judgment will fall on "us" or "them." Stuff like that. Consequently, more footnotes are needed to convey the requisite nuance.

Red Staters, by contrast, employ a conceptual model known as Moral Absolutism. This means that things rarely "depend." Fewer footnotes are needed because there is little nuance that needs conveying.

Red Staters employ their attitudes toward killing as a means to enforce rigid moral positions, for non-Christian population control, and for feeling superior.

Blue Staters employ their attitudes toward killing (or standing by, doing nothing) as a means of lifestyle management, lifespan management, Red Stater population control, and feeling superior.

**WE NOW RETURN TO OUR
REGULAR DEPROGRAMMING**

Part Seven:

SQUEEZED.
WELCOME TO THE MIDDLE.

Middlehood is a sociopolitical position that is not chosen by its occupants. It is, instead, imposed upon a group of citizens through the abuses of extremists of both conservative and liberal stripe. Many of these extremist folks are well-meaning, I suppose, but too caught up in their passion and moral certitude to notice the damage they do to the rest of us— particularly through the false, hostile dichotomy that they impose on our political discourse.

Extremists believe that we Middles are cowards who can't— or won't— take a stand. This might be a valid point if the extremists had, in fact, accurately defined the issues at hand, and correctly assessed all of the possible viewpoints, potential solutions,[1] permutations and consequences that might apply. The extremist, however, always believes that the issue is clearly articulated, and that there is but one choice to be made: are you with me, or against me? The manner in which this choice is presented never varies. You, the Middle, must decide whether you are one of the "good guys"— or an asshole.

Extremists and party loyalists heap loads of criticism, condemnation and invective— particularly around election time— on the Guy in the Middle. We are referred to as "materialistic suburban sheep," "spiritually empty and selfish," "apathetic drones mindlessly driven by advertising" and other descriptions that the extremes use to explain our baffling lack of passion about their various causes. It's part of the extremist mind-set to consider themselves both uniquely cognizant of the world's problems and defects, and uniquely in possession of the required solutions.

Unfortunately for those of us in the middle, the extremists won't leave us alone because they need *us* to reach critical mass for the deployment of their visions. That's because there are so few of them (extremists— not visions. They have visions out the wazoo.) Whether their issue is the degradation of family values, an endangered species, or capital punishment— the extremes are saddled with the frustrating and aggravating task of explaining to us numb, indifferent, self-cen-

---

1 Including the possibility that nothing can, or should be, done about it— an option no extremist can bear to contemplate.

tered Middles how blind we are to the disaster ahead. And they keep explaining it to us, over and over and over.

And of course we REFUSE TO LISTEN. So they explain it yet again. The critical idea that extremists seem to miss is that we Middles might have our own views about anything. The only things about us that seem obvious to them is that we're oblivious and in dire need of enlightenment. The result? We are doomed to an endless, torturous, forced march of attempted moral remediation from both sides.

Only the disaster rarely comes. And even when it does it is never as bad as predicted. Typically, the seers, visionaries, anointed saviors, Apostles of Doom and all the other yapping boneheads get almost all the details wrong— yet they still behave as if they alone had the prescience to See It Coming. Confirmation bias allows them to latch onto the tiniest detail they predicted correctly, regardless of triviality, and declare a victory of foresight. Like benumbed drones at the slot machines, they will keep pulling the lever of activism, hoping— believing— that the next pull will cash out.

THE MIDDLE WORLD VIEW

In addition to not being chosen by its members, Middlehood isn't a political position in the usual sense, either. It's more a random collection of all the positions that are left over after you remove the extremes of the Left and Right. Probably the common defining attribute of Middles is that, regardless of the other details of their political/social/religious views, proselytizing is not part of their *modis operandi.*

This Middle world view— held by the majority of Americans—[2] holds that "You can do whatever you want as long as it doesn't hurt me (and as long as I don't have to do it, too, unless it looks like fun), and in return, you let me do what I want, subject to the same provisions—

---

2 How do I know this? As a Middle, I actually interact with people who hold viewpoints other than mine, and must learn how to get along with them so we can work together, be neighbors, stay married, etc. Very few of us ordinary folks adhere to the world views of the extremists. Also, most of us are too polite to mow them down with the minivan just because they see things differently. Not that we don't fantasize about it.

and of course, subject to the law of the land. Also, I promise I won't try to convert you to my way of thinking because, frankly, I'm not sure my world view is infallible. Besides, I'm too busy making a living, raising a family, trying to hang on to some of my money, and waiting for the kids to grow up so I no longer have to go to Disney World on vacation."[3]

Some extremists may wonder:

"What informs this twisted, self-centered, vacuous world view of the Middle? How can they be so utterly oblivious?"

Well, I'll explain it.

If you, esteemed reader, are an Extremist, much of this may make no sense to you, although I'll do my best. If you are a Middle, you already know this stuff— so you might want to skip this section altogether and do something productive. Like, say, clean your sniper rifle.

We Middles— lacking an articulated "Capital-P" Philosophy— don't think about all this "behavior stuff" that much, so I had to look deep inside to figure out what drives this world view. This was not very difficult, because of my inherent unfathomable shallowness. Nevertheless, here are a few thoughts that I deemed worthy of sharing. I can't, of course, explain this with a high sense of Certainty, as the lack of such certainty is one of the defining characteristics of Middlehood. So, here goes, in no particular order.[4]

HARMONY.
NEVER GONNA HAPPEN.

Eons of human history illustrate that despite countless moral reformations, religious conversions and/or crusades of every type; the imposition of political correctness; widespread failed Marxist experi-

---

3 You know, a little beach house would be awfully nice, too.

4 Consistent with the rest of this book.

mentation; scores upon scores of naive utopian dreams; and all manner of other attempts to make it otherwise— people are predisposed to a set of behaviors that suggest that we're never going to all get along. Behaviors like:

- Forming groups and keeping Others out,
- Killing, maiming and raping the "Others";
- Conquering, kidnapping, torturing and enslaving whoever's left;
- Insulting and denigrating anyone who is still standing;
- Destroying the previous regime's literature, art, music, cultural heritage, and iconography— regardless of its intrinsic value;
- Abusing their own offspring;
- Starting wars for Glory, Power, Honor, Money, Revenge, Reform and/or any combination thereof;
- Stealing from the Public coffers;
- Abusing the Public Trust;
- Exploring the depths of debauchery and documenting it, at length, in every form of media from cuneiform tablets to Twitter Pics;
- Hogging resources while watching others starve;
- Soiling the nest;
- Eradicating species, leveling forests, damming rivers, etc;
- Etc, etc, etc.
- Etc.

Don't get me wrong: I love people. That doesn't mean, though, that I have to pretend that we're not wild animals. Speaking of wild animals:

NATURE IN BALANCE— A BETTER TUTOR[5]

Natural systems don't produce sustained extremes. Gravity keeps everything nicely on the ground or falling toward it. Erosion silently seeks the angle of repose. Trees don't grow trunks that are twice the girth necessary to stay up. Even a place like Antarctica, which may seem extreme to us, is a relatively stable system.[6] A pendulum may swing from side to side, but left alone will not rest at the end of its arc. Nature always seeks a state of balance, where the expenditure of energy is minimized. Rust is one example. Hounds are another.

People, however, have the ability (curse?) to override this natural inclination[7] and to try to stay out at the far ends of the arc. That, of course, is where all the drama takes place, and drama is fun. But unending drama is also very expensive psychologically, and ultimately, unsustainable.

Extremism requires the incessant output of energy just to maintain itself— never mind getting any work done. It requires the practitioner to work constantly at staying angry, fearful, enlightened, irritated, self-righteous, paranoid, or some combination of these. It's like rowing upstream. It can be done for a while, but you will get tired, and probably cranky as well.

This expenditure of energy just to stay Enlightened/Pissed robs the practitioner of the energy needed to actually get something done about whatever it is that bugs him. The more extreme a person is, the less energy gets applied to solving the problem. Eventually, these folks end up in coffee shops all night, spewing about how "nothing ever changes." (Including, they invariably fail to notice— themselves.)

Middles, on the other hand, don't use all that energy just to maintain a point-of-view. Although "floating with the current" may seem complacent to extremists, it is inherently energy-efficient and sustainable. Why bust your gut rowing when you can get the stream to do most of the work?

---

5 Note: I'm not suddenly getting all metaphysical or spiritual in this section, just using observations about nature to demonstrate a point about extremism. So, don't worry— I'm still the shallow, morally bankrupt guy you've come to know. And love (blush).

6 Yes, I know about the Wilkins ice shelf— don't start.

7 Couch-potatoes excepted.

REASONABLENESS: THE ULTIMATE GREY AREA. ICK.

Middlehood is instead fueled by the notions of reasonableness and civility. Admittedly, these are nowhere near as much fun as extremism, and you do tend to put on weight. On the other hand, your molars last longer.[8]

Reasonableness is based on the presumption that neither you nor I are going to get everything we want. Should I pause and let that sink in?

I know, I know— this is America, Land of the Whining Constituent, where everyone has an inalienable right to be free from want, live up to his fullest potential, and get a Gold Star for not waking up dead this morning. That's the perennial promise that we hear from all the True Believers. Never mind that they never deliver. *And* that it's a dumb idea.

I'm not supposed to get everything I want, and neither are you. The gap between what you want and what you get is called Ambition, and when you lose that, you are royally screwed. People who lack ambition are the ones who constantly cry about how unfair everything is. Of course it's unfair— it's Reality.

It seems strange that our culture— the one that worships sports (the embodiment of "unfair")— can be so hung up on fairness in real life. We use sports analogies such as "level playing field" to describe the way we want our system to work— not realizing just how lousy the analogy really is.

Let's take professional football. The league consists of 32 teams, each with no more than 80 players during off-season. That's 2,560 people from a nation of 308.7 million— and none of them can be women. Not even big, nasty biker-dykes can get on the gridiron. Does anything sound "level" about this so far? It gets worse. By the end of preseason, the roster must be down to 53 players (1,696 total). This

---

8 As a reformed Bruxist, I can attest to this from direct experience.

"level playing field" consists of .000005494% of the US population, so you can imagine that your basic paunchy, out-of-shape, dimwit, quasi-gimp American is never going to get on the field.

Who *is* getting on the field? Only the top .000005494% giant, rock-hard, nasty, boxcar-sized motherfuckers, that's who.[9] (Well, and some much smaller white guys— we need quarterbacks, after all.)

You aren't on a level playing field, for crissake. That's where Reason-ableness comes in. Reasonableness is the system that lets you get more than your puny talents and abilities deserve. It's the way all the rest of us mediocre specimens defeat the market forces of Ruthless Competition.[10] The more reasonable we are, the more people who get to play.

By working together and cooperating we create a better outcome for everyone— but only if each individual gives up the idea of getting everything he wants. This is nursery school stuff— why are we Ameri-cans so unclear on this?

The other pillar of the Middle world view is Civility— another laughable, quaint, sissified concept. Civility suggests that even if I don't agree with you, it is not necessary to ridicule, harass, belittle, or insult you during the process of disagreement. Civility is the Xylocaine of discourse— the pain-killer that takes away some of the sting of being wrong, and makes the dull ache of compromise more tolerable.

When adversaries work through their differences in a reasonable and civil manner, each comes away from the process a little more will-ing to try it again next time. Our current political climate does not allow this to happen. The zero-sum, black-and-white tenor of our dis-course demands that one side is deemed Right and the other Wrong— even though that view is objectively unsupportable.

I don't care which side you're on— if you look at the life you enjoy today, there are many, many aspects that make American citizenship

---

9 And a third of those are Samoan.

10 Disclosure: I was always the last kid picked for a team in gym class, which might be a formative experience for my penchant for reasonableness. This was typically expressed as "I guess we're stuck with Bourque." I lived through it with self-esteem intact. (I still cry myself to sleep sometimes …)

one of the most comfortable, fair, prosperous and safe in the world.[11] And, many, many of those aspects were contributed, and sometimes defended to the grave, by the group of people who you now call Idiots, Sinners or Infidels.

move*this*.org

In addition to the energy saved by not staying torqued up, another fuel-efficient aspect of reasonableness is that we don't need to recruit *you* to our cause in order to be successfully reasonable (or, reasonably successful, for that matter). Which is why we aren't busting your chops over the bouillabaisse. You wanna' vote for some dipshit? Fine— go ahead. When you get "governance-by-dipshit" as a result, don't complain to me about it. Now, can we serve dessert?

Middles don't need rallies, revivals, think tanks, refresher courses, webinars, pamphlets or blogs to stay informed/aware/angry about our world view. One reason? We're not inherently angry (although you extremists are really starting to grind my gears— hence this book). We don't need to seek a lot of new information to stay "current" with our Middlehood. It comes to us in endless waves.

Most important, reasonableness doesn't require victory over an opponent to function effectively. Everything about our operating system is based on compromise— we don't expect to get everything we want.

If you ascribe to an all-or-nothing philosophy— as many extremists do— that's what you'll get: sometimes all, and sometimes nothing. (It would be more accurate to call it all-and-nothing.) Let's say you get "all" half the time (which, of course, isn't really "all" at all). Winning your fair share isn't satisfying because of another cognitive inside-joke: we humans register losses more acutely than wins. So, even if you get your "fair share," you still feel like you got screwed.[12] However, if you never expected to get "all" in the first place, there's no letdown.

---

11 No, we're not perfect. We never will be. Get over it.

12 Assuming, of course, that all you wanted was your fair share. Right.

REASONABLENESS NOW— OR ELSE!

A rally of Middles would not be front-page material. CNN® probably wouldn't cover it because the rally would never take place— we're too busy. But even if somehow we managed to get time off from work, find baby sitters, board the pets, and take care of all the other details that would allow us to March on Washington (even that would be difficult— "After you." "Oh, I couldn't possibly— you were here first." "I insist"), what would we march about? Imagine the signs:

> "Let's think things over!"
>
> "You might have a point, there."
>
> "Yo, Yo— Quid Pro Quo!"
>
> "Tolerance NOW!"
>
> "You scratch mine, I'll scratch yours!"
>
> "Two, four, six, eight; I'm an angry moderate!"
>
> "On the other hand …!"

Million Man schlep?

WHY ARE WE SO MAD AT RICH PEOPLE?

Meet one of the few people in America who doesn't envy or hate Bill Gates. That's correct: I don't have a problem with Bill Gates.[13] As far as I can tell, he didn't do anything wrong to anyone. The guy saw the computer revolution coming, and did something about it. Sure, he made a crummy interface (I've been an Apple Person from day one.[14]), but you don't have to buy it. If you don't like Microsoft, don't give them your money. Code your own damn operating system, slacker.

On the other hand, he was instrumental in creating an industry that employs a gazillion people, many in the Third World, which has

---

13 Of course, as you will see below, I don't hate Starbucks, either, so what would you expect?

14 Shameless plug. Maybe Apple will sponsor me.

made a whole universe of information available to anyone with just a few keystrokes— important information, such as pornography from anywhere on the globe. Do you have any idea how difficult it was to get Inuit porno before the Internet?

Anyway, this hatred of rich people comes from Zero-Sum Thinking (as covered in Section Three): if Bill Gates has a septilio-fuckload of money, and I have none, he must have screwed me out of my rightful share. It's not "fair." But Bill Gates isn't an unmotivated, sniveling, self-absorbed slouch with a hangover— like those of us who are doing all the complaining. Nothing is stopping any one of us from being at the Right Place at the Right Time, with the knowledge, energy and insight to do something that will Profoundly Change the World Forever.[15]

I realize that what I'm about to say is not going to be popular, but here goes anyway: Rich people do not owe the rest of us jack shit.[16] This notion that we should decide how much money someone else "needs" is arrogant and offensive. Try using that same reasoning about something other than wealth and it becomes obvious just how outrageous it is.

Let's say that you are an extraordinarily talented musician. Should we take some of your talent and give it to someone else who doesn't have any? Maybe you have a face that could launch a thousand ships. Nothing a little acid couldn't fix. You should be as ugly as the rest of us— it's not fair. Possibly you're six-foot-fourteen and destined for a soaring career in basketball. Let's saw off your legs at mid shin— that will make it more "equitable."

Nobody would suggest that we confiscate someone's talent and give it to someone else— primarily because it's not possible. When it comes to money, that's another story entirely— because it *is* possible. Money is one thing that we can confiscate from others who "have too

---

15 Note: being drunk at 2:00 PM on Sunday in a sports bar is probably not the best place to wait for Opportunity to come knocking. Just a thought.

16 Disclaimer: I am not rich, poised to inherit a fortune, Oprah's secret lover, a Microsoft stockholder, or in any way an apologist for the wealthy. I just believe it's their goddam' money.

much." Therefore, one of the most important functions of government is larceny. Oops. I meant: "redistribution of wealth."

Some people have a formula for the "proper" ratio of an executive's compensation to that of everyone else in the organization. This idea is typically expressed as "No executive should be allowed to earn more than X times that of the lowliest line-worker"[17, 18]

Allowed? I suppose the best goat-herder on the Sahel shouldn't be allowed to accumulate in excess of X more nannies than the worst one. How about ceramicists? Too many pots? We'll just take those, thank you very much.

This is getting interesting. Let's "redistribute" grade points in our schools. Chad, over here in the Deke House, is averaging a 1.3, despite his valiant efforts to better himself through intensive cannabis and alcohol therapy— whereas Melody, across campus in the Physics Lab, is about to capture a neutrino in a lipstick cap and Fedex it to Stephen Hawking as a birthday gift. Her GPA currently stands at 11.4783452.

Well, that's just not fair. We'll just "level" those: let's see, that's 6.3891726 for each of them— well above the national average, if not the actual GPA scale itself.

Next, let's ask ourselves: Who got screwed in this arrangement? Melody still has a GPA high enough to prevent her from getting married, and Chad has opportunities once denied him because of Society's Intolerance of his Cultural Beliefs. Only Hawking— who has spent his entire life trying to get a neutrino of his own— has lost out, but he will never know this because Melody missed the Fedex pickup while she was at the Administration Building vainly attempting to discover what the hell happened to her grades.[19] So— no harm, no foul. And "Social Justice" has occurred!

---

17   Also known by the Nounjetive: HardWorkingAmerican.

18   Keith Olberman recently "left" MSNBC. Word is they paid him $7 million a year, which works out to $3,365 bucks an hour. What do you suppose was the ratio between his compensation and that of the "lowliest line worker" at MSNBC? Well, production assistants get $15 an hour. So, that ratio is about 224-to-1.

19   Chad later won a gender-discrimination lawsuit against the university, resulting in the confiscation of grade points from 236 undergraduate and 62 postgraduate women, as well as the nullification of the doctorates of 9 female faculty members.

The fact is, we could take all of Bill's dough and spread it around to those who think he has "too much" and they wouldn't be any happier— why? Because they're not happy people.

YOU THOUGHT THAT WAS BAD …

I like Starbucks.

There, I said it. I hope they sell my book in their stores. I like Starbucks for precisely the reasons some other people think they are Evil Incarnate: I like them because they are ALL EXACTLY THE FRIGGIN' SAME. Given that I'm already foolish enough to pay three-and-a-half bucks for a cup of coffee, I want to make certain that I don't get hosed out of my money because some nut-job wants to express his political views in my cup.

I can go to any Starbucks, anywhere on Earth, and know that my Skinny Vanilla Latté[20] is going to taste just the way I expect it to. Whenever I can't find a Starbucks and have to go to some "independent" coffee house, I get royally screwed. Here's why:

The Coffee House Bitterness Index (CHBI)

The CHBI holds that the bitterness of the coffee in a given establishment is directly correlated with the bitterness of the people who inhabit it. In broad strokes, coffee is milder and sweeter in the suburbs and reaches its peak bitterness on college campuses. In the 'burbs, people meet for coffee to get away from the irritations of daily life— kids, laundry, asshole bosses, school officials, and people knocking on their doors promoting some agenda. So the coffee is mild and sweet— an indulgence savored for a few precious moments before returning to Hell.

At the other end of the continuum, college students gather at the local independent coffee shop to escape the boredom of schoolwork

---

20 No, I'm not gay.

and review with their friends all the things about the world that make them angry and bitter. So, the coffee needs to be some awful, vile swill that reinforces the bitterness of their reality, while helping fund micro-loans in some Third World country where the Corrupt U.S. government is Trading Blood for Oil. From what I can tell, growing coffee in the shade makes it bitter and angry.

I'm starting to sound bitter and angry myself. It's true— I'm sick of these people.

WELCOME TO THE MIDDLE—
YOUR TURN TO BREATHE IS COMING UP.

So here is where we "ordinary" folks find ourselves: smashed between these two self-appointed groups of social engineers/moral reformers who are battling over who should run our lives. We didn't agree to this, and we don't recognize them as experts or authorities. They're "not the boss of us," yet we're always receiving orders from them— which, of course, we are studiously trying to ignore. The more we try to ignore them, the more "effort redoubling" they apply, and so on.

People in the middle live a life of give-and-take: they know from experience things that idealists never seem to understand. They know that surviving in America requires a mixture of conservativeness in certain areas and liberalness in others, and that the proportion changes continually. It makes sense to be conservative when you have something to protect such as your children, your home or your culture. Other times, it makes sense to behave in a liberal manner, such as when you need to function as a member of a community made of people with varying needs and agendas.

Most people I know are a mixture of conservative, moderate and liberal— depending on circumstance. The convenient labels of Conservative and Liberal are inaccurate lies about the kind of people we really are. The use of these terms creates the false impression that the person described is essentially one-dimensional— when most of us are much more complex and significantly less rigid than the labels suggest.

Liberals can be "conservative" sometimes— and vice-versa. If, for example, an ethnic minority which is widely considered to be of a liberal bent, works to keep its cultural heritage intact within a larger culture, it is engaging in conservative behavior. It's *conserving* its culture against the pressures to conform to the dominant culture. This has happened all over the world, and throughout history. Further, by demanding tolerance by the larger culture, it is asking for *liberal* behavior from the larger group. And by the way, if the larger group works to keep its cultural heritage intact as well, it is not *per se* engaging in repression, although it is quite popular to accuse them of it. It might be engaging in similar conservative behavior to preserve its *own* cultural heritage. Simply being the majority does not automatically confer repressive motives.

Even if you are an ultraprogressive with an exciting new agenda who wants to start a revolution, you will discover what always happens once the revolution succeeds: you will become more conservative. It happens to every revolutionary because after you've won, you must protect (conserve) your hard-won investment against assaults from new groups of idealistic progressive reformers. Many of these will remind you of yourself "back in the day". But they're not part of your new ruling class, and they want your hide. Study history. What nearly always follows Liberation? Ruthless, murderous repression.

If, on the other hand, you're an ultraconservative, don't forget that nearly all the rights and freedoms you enjoy as an American had to be fought for— wrenched away through violence from oppressors who were trying to conserve *their* way of life. Many people who are asking for change today are motivated by the same passion. If they can't have a fair shake, you will find yourself on the wrong side of the revolution— like George III.

Being a Middle in America these days is like driving a minivan with two squabbling children in the back: they won't shut up no matter what you say; they're out of arm's reach so you can't slap the shit out of them; and you no longer Give a Fuck Who Started It.

Well, I'm afraid I have bad news: there's no sign that these two political spoiled brats are going to stop the squabbling anytime soon. Therefore, we have no recourse but to learn how to better cope.

Part Eight:

COPING STRATEGIES FOR MIDDLES

If you're still with me at this point, you may be a Middle yourself. Either that, or you are an Extremist with a penchant for being insulted. Let's assume you are a fellow Middle.

In this section we will explore some coping mechanisms that you, oppressed Middle, can use to make life more tolerable in this jacked-up, partisan screechfest that we call America. But first— some context.

CAN'T WE ALL JUST GET ALONG?

No. Sorry.

Despite Rodney King's plaintive plea (slightly paraphrased), we can't. Why? Because we hate one another's guts.

You already knew that, didn't you?

We humans have a shocking level of disregard for everything around us— the environment, other species, international borders, virginity, property rights, peace and quiet, law and order, fairness, equality, morality, personal hygiene, good taste and self-dignity, to name but a few.

But we save a special place in our collective shriveled little heart for our fellow *homo sapiens.* We will maim, enslave and slaughter one another for the most appalling and often trivial reasons: for ascribing to a different creed; to steal property; to save the fetuses; to save the little bunnies; because our parents slaughtered Hatfields/McCoys/Serbs/ Hutus/Apaches/Jews/Christians/Muslims; because they buggered our sheep. And we love doing it.

Let's be honest— that's exactly why we just can't stop killing, raping, mauling, cheating, and everything-else-ing one another.

Ever notice that there's no Society For The Prevention Of Cruelty To Humans, or People for the Ethical Treatment of Each Other? That's because no one would join. Save the bunnies? —Hell yes. Save the "others"? —Fuck that noise.

Yet, despite the preponderance— the mountain— the avalanche— the torrent— damn, there's just no word big enough— the obliteratingly cataclysmic, mind-numbing, infinitely powerful bludgeon of evidence that suggests that we are never going to "all get along," there are still people out there who are going to give it a whirl anyway. Those people drive me nuts.

THERE ARE TWO KINDS OF PEOPLE IN THIS WORLD; THOSE WHO DIVIDE PEOPLE INTO GROUPS, AND THOSE WHO DON'T.

I'M IN THE SECOND GROUP.[1]

It's a nice sentiment that somehow we can all just get along and see each person for the beautiful, creative, loving individual huddled inside instead of the short/tall/black/white/brown/male/female/straight/gay/Christian/Muslim/Animist/Wiccan on the outside, but the facts seem to indicate that humans like to sort themselves into groups— usually some version of 'Us' and 'Them'.

The ideas of "Us" and "Them" are too deeply rooted in us to overcome. We're tribal. Deep down, "Us" is really an extension of "Me," and I hope like hell there isn't a movement starting on some college campus to make it discriminatory for me to notice that I am "me" and everyone else is, well— everyone else. I'd be the first to be accused of "selfism." I do, in fact, discriminate against everyone who isn't me. So do you.

Nevertheless, an enormous amount of thought, talk and effort has been spent trying to persuade us that these differences don't exist, but try as they may, the PC Police can't get people to stop noticing these differences and pretend that everyone is a wonderful addition to the human race. We Middles know this is crap. Not all people are wonderful inside. Some of them are really quite despicable. Perhaps you know some of these:

---

1 This is a mangled version of a quote from Robert Benchley.

- Pedantic, overbearing asshole
- Niggling, interfering bitch
- Dreadlocked, unemployed pseudo intellectual
- Lazy, sneering, negative slacker
- Sexist, drooling, leering coworker
- Nouveau-riche, preening yuppie
- Sinewy, glowing, spandex-clad, fitness junkie
- Ass-grabbing, bullying frat boy
- Egotistic, pomaded, self-appointed messiah
- Rancid, butt-crack showing, dumb, drunk yahoo
- Larcenous, oily little shit
- Self-loathing, whiny, emotional sniveler
- Self-published social critic

See my point? I'll bet you can think of some, too.

Besides, even those who believe they are completely blind to race, age, gender, creed, sexual orientation, height, weight and every other possible human differentiating factor are nonetheless faced with the fact that some others still aren't. That means that until every human on the planet is converted to rainbow-coalition political correctness, there will still be, at minimum, two groups: the converted and the unconverted. (Realistically, there will always be more than that due to the inevitable splinter-group problem. Some people, for example, will be long-term, second- and third-generation "openness practitioners," while others will be those irritating "Nouveau-PC types" who are just in it for the Moral Extra Credit. Next thing you know there are two mailing lists, certain people get invited to the better protests, resumes get compared, etc.).

So, I'm saying that we Middles need to just face the facts, and, to recap, those facts are:

- People are never going to stop being malevolent, tribal animals;
- Some people are never going to stop trying to "reform" us anyway.

COPING STRATEGIES

Because extremists are incorrigible, we are going to be assaulted with all sorts of annoying partisan pressure, and there's no sign of it letting up any time soon. So we're going to need to learn to cope. Herewith are a few guidelines and techniques to make the paddling line of life a little more tolerable.

STEP ONE: EVALUATE THE PRESENTER.

One way to save yourself a lot of misery and wasted time is to quickly evaluate whether you should listen to even one friggin' word that gets uttered by the person presenting the Big Idea. Here are some speedy ways to determine whether you should immediately disqualify your presenter and exit the room.

Is he presenting something?— If I have the key to eternal happiness, wealth, wisdom or anything else valuable, I'm going to keep it a secret, so I can keep all of it. If I'm presenting it to you, it must not be worth shit. Yet, I still want you to pay good money for it. This book, for example: have you ever encountered such a collection of worthless drivel?

Did *he* bring up the subject?— When was the last time a neurologist approached you on the street and asked if he could hit your knee with that little tomahawk thingy and give you a free diagnosis? Exactly.

Does he exhibit any of the qualities he's selling?— Of course not. He's a twisted, smelly, disheveled, and/or poverty-stricken wretch who's trying to get you to validate his appalling choices in life by buying into all his nonsense.

La Prison Liberté— Beware of anyone who is going to "Liberate" you:

Marx	Guevara
Tito	Mugabe
Castro	Chavez
Jong-Il	Robespierre
Mussolini	Amin
Pinochet	Hitler
Minh	Mobutu
Peron	Pot
Bokassa	Duvalier

Redeem This— Beware of anyone who is going to "Save" you:

Jones	Karesh
Hubbard	Moon
Applewhite	Etc, *ad nauseum* …

Beware of "Visionaries"— Many, many extremists will present themselves this way. Don't fall for it. Anyone who is willing to introduce himself as a visionary— isn't. Here are some basic rules that must apply to the awarding of the term:

- You can't award it to yourself;
- You have to wait at least until the future you are predicting actually arrives, *and* turns out to be the way you predicted it;
- If thousands of ordinary people also correctly predicted it, it doesn't count;
- If one moron also correctly predicted it, it doesn't count;
- The title should only be awarded posthumously, so you never hear yourself labeled as one.

STEP TWO: EVALUATE THE PRESENTATION.

OK, somehow you screwed up, the doors are locked and the "Brief, 15-minute Presentation" has begun. You can still defend yourself. Below are some concepts and techniques that you can use while under attack, that will allow you to keep your skepticism without the need to either listen to the arguments or absorb any "facts" in the presentation.

The Inverse-Certainty Rule— This rule holds that you should apply skepticism in direct proportion to the certainty of the speaker. Plenty (way too many, if you ask me) of people will get behind the podium and tell you they have the answers. Before you lay down your money, your allegiance, your virginity or anything else of value, take a good look at the person espousing the Big Concept. Is this the Alan Greenspan of morality/political strategy/world-saving or whatever it is that's being espoused?[2] If not, assume that the espouser has a personal reason to convince you of his Concern *du Jour*. Run, before you become yet another victim of espousal abuse. The reason you can be unilaterally skeptical of Certainty is:

The Fluctuation Constant— Fluctuation is permanent. What is not permanent is the rate of fluctuation— it fluctuates. Because of this, no one can predict anything accurately— particularly experts, who could be described fairly as people who are willing to make predictions despite the fact that it is an appalling bad idea. So there is no such thing as Certainty.

The Immutable Law of Gray Area— There is one thing that you can bank on in life; one thing that is absolutely, positively true— one thing that you can be utterly Certain about— and that is: nothing is ever black and white. Each type of extremist copes with this Law differently, depending on which side of the aisle he sits. Ultraconservatives respond to this by looking for a higher authority like God to sort it all out for them, and then rely on that explanation pretty much forever. Ultraliberals cope by declaring themselves God, by virtue of their all-powerful intellect, and then

---

2 Keep in mind that Alan Greenspan himself didn't turn out to be the Alan Greenspan of his milieu.

make all the relativistic judgment calls as they go. Both systems ignore the vast grayness of the reality that we Middles inhabit.

The fractal nature of reality— In simplistic terms, a fractal is a form that has an essentially identical shape no matter how far you zoom in or out. If you were floating in space, the edge of a land-mass would look all squiggly and crinkly. If you swooped down to a mile high, the edge would look pretty much the same— squiggly and crinkly. Zoom in further— more squig and crink, all the way down to a square inch of edge— or even the molecular level. Squig. Crink.

Many of us have seen those fractal generators that came with our PCs a while back, which got a bunch of computer geek/virgins inexplicably excited. Those are graphic representations of the idea of a fractal.

Anyway, reality is like that, too. However finely you divide something, there's still enough space between the parts to divide it again, and again. Forever. (See: Politicians, Agents of Change, in Part 6.) Let's say your presenter sets up his whole spiel by defin-ing the "two ways" you can look at the subject at hand: His Way, and, of course; the Wrong Way. That's a nice attempt to define the debate, I suppose. But there are a hell of a lot more than those "two ways" to look at a thing. There are gazillions— with gazillions more between those. ...

Consult the Ca-Ching— Although this sounds like an obscure Eastern philosophy of some sort, it is much simpler than that, and involves only the answer to one question: Is your money involved? If the answer is "yes," and that involvement consists of your mon-ey flowing out of your account and into someone else's— be ex-tremely skeptical.

Tug on the harness— Are you allowed to exit the presentation any time you want to? If the answer is "no", it is acceptable to hurt someone in order to escape.

Last-resort solution: The Presentation Mantra— Here is a technique you can use if all else fails. Just close your eyes and silently repeat this mantra to yourself until the presentation is over: "getmethefuckouttaheregetmethefuckouttaheregetmethefuckout- taheregetmethefuckouttaheregetmethefuckouttahere ..."

SOME GENERAL RULES

If you are the subject of a presentation ("dialogue") that is either, by some miracle, finely nuanced, or— more likely— so long-winded that you cannot discern The Point, there are a number of tools you can employ early in the presentation to detect that you are being sold a bill of goods. These can be held, at the ready, in your brain as a kind of distant early warning system.

Avoid institutions that offer both the disease and the cure— Most religions fall into this category. First, they define everything interesting and fun as a Sin, then teach you how to feel guilty and dirty about it, and last, offer coping mechanisms for the ensuing guilt and self-loathing— mechanisms available only through the institution that makes you feel like shit in the first place. It's a system that results in a very profitable vicious cycle— one in which you are the cycle, and the institution is going to viciously ride you all the way to the bank.

A good way to tell if the proselytizer of the moment is selling one of these systems is to take note of the process by which he informs you. Does it begin with a series of questions designed to get you to admit that you are unhappy, poor, frustrated, downtrodden, victimized, unappreciated, or in some way getting the short end of the stick?[3] If so, the next part is where he informs you of the cure, and the fact that he knows it and you don't. Make sure you escape before he gets to that part.

Sancti-Money— Huge profits are to be made in the sancti- mony business, which is why so many extremists practice it. If you

---

3 Of course you are unhappy, poor, frustrated, downtrodden, victimized, unappreciated, or in some way getting the short end of the stick, unless you happen to be Brangelina, The Donald, Oprah, Bono, or someone like that. If you are one of those people— I'll bet you're not reading this.

are being pressured to join some sort of movement that makes its leaders rich or powerful in the name of some noble cause, get out of the room now.

Sancti-Honey— If the leader gets to doink all the chicks, that's another Cause you don't want to join. (Unless you're a chick, and you like that sort of thing. Still, I'll wager that it doesn't work out for you in the long run.)

Reject the binary discourse— Remember that the subject, tone and rancor level of nearly all political discourse in our society is determined, presented and repeated by people who have a vested interest in the dialogue being horrible. This includes politicians, pundits, media people, campaign volunteers, and individual activists. None of these people want a civilized discourse, because they always— and only— want to win the debate. The only way for the Middle to escape the system is to refuse to participate.

Remember that these TWO WAYS of looking at the world are artificially supported, mutually exclusive world views that have been presented to us as the only possibilities for so long that we have forgotten that there might be other ways to look at things. A third way.[4] And a fourth, fifth, sixth and infinitely more ways. What's yours?

Don't accept this artificial Red/Blue divide— it's bullshit. The divide in our discourse should fall along a different line: Reasonable vs. Extreme. Instead of half the country (red) feeling angry and marginalized half the time, and the other half (blue) feeling that way the other half of the time— how about this:

Let's make the extremists feel angry and marginalized *all the time,* and see that their contribution to the national dialogue shrinks to the tiny slice that accurately represents both their proportion of the population and their actual potential contribution to any plausible solutions to anything.

I will admit that it won't make for entertaining talk shows (Bill Maher will need to look for real work under this system), but I

---

4 No, not that "Third Way"—Flee!

believe it would be better for most of us. Imagine— all us Middles banding together and ignoring the fringies and fundamentalists until they finally wheeze themselves to death. It's a picture of a Golden Future, I say.

Refuse to engage extremists in dialogue— It's easy to get caught up in their agenda because they typically start conversations by pissing you off with some outrageous nonsense. Resist the impulse to defend yourself. Remember that confrontation is their hobby— they LOVE engaging in this crap. Every minute you spend "conversing" with an extremist is a minute lost from your life— a minute you could spend on something important and valuable TO YOU.

When an Idealist or True Believer tries to engage you in dialogue, it is not because he wants to improve your life. He wants to improve something about himself that requires your participation to achieve. Behave as if he were holding you up at gunpoint— because he is trying to rob you of moments of your life for his purposes. Dialogue with extremists *always* benefit the extremist— *never* you.

Stop watching the news— In 2008, we finished an eight-year news cycle, which included as one of its principal features, a continuous effort to scare the crap out of Americans about the economy. We had been hearing dire warnings about an imminent recession from the Left and the media since 2000, when the Bushies took over. According to the group that monitors such things, the recession "officially" started in December 2007. That is seven years of the media harping about The Recession Boogeyman before it actually took place.

No, I am not saying that the Media created the recession. However, since the economic behavior of our citizens affects the economy at least as much as government policy, it is impossible to rule out the possibility of the media's role in creating a self-fulfilling prophecy by scaring our citizens into behavior not in our collective best interest.

I don't expect the media to be unbiased— who is? But wishing for, and possibly helping create, an economic disaster because you hate the politics of a sitting President should be considered an act of Treason. People's livelihoods and futures are at stake. Fourth Estate my ass.

Earlier we looked behind the curtain of Conspiracy Theory, where I took the position that it is usually unnecessary. Here is a wonderful example of why a conspiracy is not needed to achieve a commonly held purpose. It is simply unnecessary for politicians, pundits, the media and all the other interested parties to hold secret meetings to review strategy for monopolizing the airwaves, because each party has a vested self-interest driving their participation. They each fall naturally into their roles— without any formal structure. Just as the automakers and oil companies do.

HOW FAST SHOULD YOU HEAD FOR THE EXIT?

A good way to determine your retreat speed when dealing with someone who's engaging you in "dialogue" is to ignore most of what they say and look for the "bottom line" of their pitch.

"We have the answers."

Run. As fast as you can.

"We have all the questions, and all the people who can figure out the answers."

Walk briskly. Guard your wallet.

"We have some of the questions, need help in defining more of them, realize we will never get it all figured out, and most important— need everyone's participation in the solutions. And, by the way, it's going to be a lot of hard work."

This will rarely happen, but if it does, sit down and get to know these folks. They might get something accomplished.

LOYAL OPPOSITION

During the formation of this great country of ours, our Founding Fathers[5] practiced a principle known as Loyal Opposition. The idea behind this is simple, yet it could have significant positive implications for discourse and effective communication. Here's how it works, expressed as a Preamble:

> We, the members of the Founding Fathers/Joint Chiefs/School Board/ Condo Association, etc.— may disagree about certain aspects of the tasks that we have undertaken, and about the details of how we're going to accomplish them, but there exists among us an overarching agreement that we are all working toward a shared goal, which is more important than our individual needs.

This idea of a shared, higher goal made it possible for these brave men to rise above their petty interests[6] and create the longest-lasting sort-of-non-totalitarian[7] government in history, bestowing upon us the rights and freedoms (that we each eventually acquired, at different times, and to varying degrees) that all of us take completely for granted today.

This principle of Loyal Opposition had vanished by the third Presidential election in 1797, and has not been seen since.

I'm suggesting that we take another whack at it.[8] In fact, in my snarky, witty and otherwise deeply compelling wrap-up and closing rant, I have some suggestions to this end. It's coming up soon, and you'll love it— but, no skipping!

---

5 A group of white, male, sexist, racist, warlike, hegemonistic pricks.

6 Sexism, racism, war, hegemony and other pricky stuff.

7 Everyone, including the President in his latest *State of the Union* Address, refers to the U.S. as a Democracy. We're not. We are a Republic. Or we used to be, anyway.

8 I'm just a crazy, starry-eyed idealist, I guess …

Wait … my snarky, witty and otherwise deeply compelling wrap-up and closing rant is, in fact, the next section of the book! There's no need to suffer in anticipation after all.

Ready? Pucker up!

Part Nine:

CLOSING RANT AND DRESSING-DOWN

A "DIALOGUE" WITH THE AUTHOR

I think I have been pretty darned civil up to this point, but that is about to change. In this section, I am going to tell off these fringie whack-jobs once and for all. How you as a reader will react to the following section depends on what kind of person you are:

If you're a Middle, I hope to say some things that you would also like to get off your chest, and that the following screed will give you a glimmer of solace and relief.

If you are an extremist and/or a True Believer, perhaps the following section will give you some idea how awful it is to interact with you.

So, hey— let's get going!

We are about to engage in a "dialogue," which you should expect— if you have already read the section on Operational Methodologies— to consist entirely of me talking and you listening.[1]

I'M MAD AS HELL— AND BLABBITY, BLATHER, SPEW!

Every election year that passes, we Middles have to endure another torrent of horseshit from you two self-appointed groups of social engineers/moral reformers who are battling to determine who gets to run our lives. The entirety of our political discourse is determined by you guys: a bunch of loudmouth jerkwads who each have some cancerous personal/moral/social agenda that is primarily focused on making you feel better about yourselves, regardless of the cost to civility, fairness, freedom, the economy, our mutual future or the public good.

Aided by members of the media who are also enthusiastic partners in this process, reasonable people are presented only with your distorted, hyperdramatic, paranoid scenarios intended to scare the crap out of us and create an affected, false, nasty, rancorous two-party dichotomy that drives reason, thoughtfulness, compromise, shared pur-

---

1 Of course this is a book, so how could it be otherwise? To make this more realistic, pretend that you have just answered your doorbell on an otherwise lovely Saturday afternoon.

pose and common sense out of the public dialogue.

Political parties respond to this environment by presenting candidates who appeal to this phony, shrieking class-war mentality, resulting in choices that, frankly, suck.[2]

All of you— extremists and media alike— have a vested interest in preserving and supporting this climate of hate because that's how you make a living. Because you are a small slice of the population— and you know it— you find it necessary to con, frighten and bully the rest of us into supporting your agenda to insure your survival. To that end, you invent fear-based scenarios, distribute lies about your opponents, and spend BILLIONS[3] of dollars pummeling the rest of us to get your guys in office. Where, on balance, they don't do shit.

Deep inside, your worst fear is that the rest of us will wake up one morning, experience a moment of clarity, and tell all of you to fuck off.

Well, I'm just one guy, but what the heck?

Fuck off.

You are driving us nuts, and we're not interested in listening while you outline your plans for us. Here are some reasons we Middles want you jerks to give up the pursuit of our hearts and minds:

You don't know anything about us. The principal reason is that neither of you believe that understanding us is necessary. You don't need to know *us* because you already "know better." Every time you try to "help" us, you screw with our lives— mostly because you don't think we should be consulted. Then you move on to the next project and leave us behind to clean up the mess.

Your track records suck. Why should we adopt your belief system/philosophy/lifestyle when it doesn't even work for you? Where are all your success stories? Fundamentalist righties seem to have astonishing difficulty keeping their morals under control, despite all the righteous

---

2 I know, I know— Obama was different.

3 Yeah, Obama is different. A goal of a BILLION dollars to re-elect a sitting President.

rhetoric. Want to know if your fundamentalist preacher is a closeted homo bone-smoker? Listen to his sermons— if he's railing against gays all the time, you can take it to the bank. And why do you need to go to a rally to understand how to be a good husband and father? Isn't all that stuff already covered in your Holy Book? Or common fucking sense?

The Left, on the other hand, has been reforming everything it can get its hands on in America for at least a hundred years and the schools still stink, women still dress like sex objects (even young girls. *Really* young girls), members of the various races still hate one another, people still try to accumulate "unneeded" wealth, poverty has been far from eradicated, and most folks try to live among people who are more like them than not. The only things that have changed are the terms we use to describe the people we abhor moving into the neighborhood.

The experts you quote are your cronies. Why are we supposed to be convinced by the testimony of other nut cases who believe the same things you do? Mass hysteria doesn't equate to Truth. If your idea doesn't make sense to me, it's not going to start just because some yahoo repeats the same crap on TV.

Quoting your "Holy Book" doesn't convince us of anything. I don't care if it's the Holy Bible, Qur'an, Mother Jones, National Review, Mein Kampf, Wired or The Anarchist Cookbook— if you're a frothing partisan, I assume everything you tell me is slanted, unattributable bullshit until proved otherwise. Your Holy Book is the fount of your belief system, to which— as you might recall— I don't ascribe. Why do you think jamming chapter and verse up my ass is going to change my mind?

Very few of you have real jobs. Middles don't listen to lobbyists, social commentators, talk-show hosts, fundamentalists, utopians, socialists, activists, politicians, spin doctors or unemployed know-it-all hippies.[4] We listen to people who work and produce something tangible instead of unwanted, self-righteous criticism or ratings-grabbing chatter.

---

4 Full disclosure: when I was young, I was an unemployed know-it-all hippie, but not for long. The pay stinks.

We're not your lab animals. Sorry, science class is dismissed: get a life. How did you get the idea that the rest of us are just waiting breathlessly for your advice? To put it politely— bugger off.

Most of you are self-righteous, narrow-minded, hypocritical pedantic assholes. Does this item really need a paragraph of elaboration? Thought not.

We're more afraid of *you* than your apocalypse. We don't listen to you because your cure is so often worse than the disease. No matter what problem you're trying to solve, calamity you're hoping to convince us is imminent, or looming horror to which you think we're oblivious— the solution always seems to involve *you* being in charge, and *us* taking orders. And taking them up the patootie.

Did you enjoy that? We're not finished. Here are some "suggestions" of ways that you could Profoundly Change Your Life that would Make The World a Better Place (for we Middles).

Stop "Helping" us. Helping people without their permission and/or participation is an act of effrontery, and is taken by Middles as a declaration of war. Mind your own fucking business.

Stop lecturing us. You are neither intellectually nor morally superior to us, and your "advice" is unwanted and unheeded for a number of reasons, including, but not limited to, the following:

- We don't accept you as experts.

- Your agenda taints your advice.

- Your results don't command respect.

- We know you desperately need us to complete your agenda, so we view you with deep suspicion.

- You have shown repeatedly that you don't really care about us.

- We didn't request assistance.

You are more self-righteous than the Deity you claim to serve. We have a major problem with that.

Lead by example and shut up. If your way of life is so superior, why don't you just live it and wait for everyone to notice how much better off you seem to be? Then, pop a Bud and sit at home while we all beat a path to your door begging for The Secret. Hell, charge us for it— you'll get rich. However, if you notice that no one has shown up, consider the following explanations:

- We have seen your example and want nothing to do with it.
- Your superiority is a figment of your imagination and, consequently, invisible to the rest of us.
- Your creed is worse that the ones we already follow.
- Your spouse writes a blog about what a jackass you actually are behind closed doors.[5]

Get a job and a life. I promise, you'll be way too busy to tell me what to do.

Learn some history. Whatever your "Big Idea", it's already been tried— many times. Figure out why it always fails and then, when you present your Bold New Plan, make sure it has some important aspects that are different from the last umpteen failed attempts. Otherwise, keep hittin' the books.

Read something besides your bible(s). You're stewing your brain in that shit. Get a second opinion.

How does that make you feel? Not very warm and fuzzy if you're a True Believer, I'll bet. Well, that's what it's like listening to you. Don't get up, though— there's one more round. Here are some reasons we Middles are not trying to impose our ways on you:

We are more tolerant than you are. We are willing to let you live in peace even if we don't agree with or understand you.[6]

---

5 Not only that, your spouse's blog, unlike yours, actually has a following.

6 Of course we understand you all too well— primarily because you NEVER shut up.

We don't need you to advance our agenda. There are plenty of us, we always have critical mass, and we aren't looking for any advisors, thank you very much.

It would never occur to us that we should be empowered to boss you around. We are too busy managing our own lives to take you on as a project.

We don't need rallies, campaigns and media buys to bolster our "moderateness." One of the beauties of Middlehood is that it is the very definition of a sustainable system. Middles don't need support groups, marches on Washington, newsletters, blogs, revivals, or documentaries to either attract new members or help us "keep the faith." It's astonishingly easy— we just get up in the morning.

We don't claim to have Certainty. Why? Because it's preposterous and arrogant. Reality is unfathomable— get over it.

Did I say "one more round" earlier? I lied. Sucks, don't it? That's another thing you do that's irritating. You're always promising "a short, 15-minute presentation" before we get our cruise tickets— then you trap us in the Sales Office for some double-teaming. Now it's your turn:

GET BENT
(This hurts me more than it hurts you.)

We don't need a rigid moral or political creed because we can figure it out as we go— and the way things are going lately, "figuring-it-out-as-you-go" is the only coping strategy that makes any sense to us. This attitude drives you both nuts, but we're not going to accept your ways when ours so obviously works better— at least for us. However, we're willing to respect your choice to do things your way as well. Please return the favor.

You idealists and extremists are doomed to live in a perpetual state of disappointment and frustration. Because you have set goals and expectations that can't be met, your struggle to achieve those goals is never-ending. We aren't ever going to have a society where everything is fair, sin-free, color-blind, equitable, moral, lawful or whatever you have your hearts set on. You can't accept this.

Middles, on the other hand, are prepared to accept a standard of pretty-darn-good/most of the time, because we understand that reality is a chaotic, fractal, ever-changing, uncontrollable mess that can't be tamed by force of human will— ever. So we work with reality— not against it.

You keep explaining (and explaining) to us How Things Are, but your story doesn't match our observations. And you simply will not stop.

Well, this is my country, too, and I am getting sick of this bullshit. You two are screwing up our society through your collective bigotry, closed-mindedness, sanctimony, intolerance, self-centered world views and unending hypocrisy. Neither of you has all the answers, and much of what you believe is, at minimum, the product of flawed reasoning, and at worst, whole-cloth nonsense.

We need ALL of us— not just your half— and we need to find common purpose, whatever that might be. I don't claim to know the answer to that question, but I do know this: anyone who is trying to "win" at citizenship is not going to contribute anything positive to the process or the outcome.

To the Right:

Change is inevitable. You cannot stop it. Stop trying. The good news is that change is slow, so you'll have time to adjust. Take a breath.

To the Left:

Change is slow. Stop trying to push it. You can't. The good news is that change is inevitable, so you don't need to work so hard to make it happen. Reality will take care of that. Take up a hobby or something.

To both of you:

- You are not going to get everything you want.
- You are not supposed to get everything you want.
- It's not *good for you* to get everything you want.
- Get used to it.

Whew! I need a cigarette— and I don't even smoke.

Back in a minute.

Boy, do I feel better.

Where do we go from here? I've had my little rant, and insulted just about everyone by this point. Well, like any true believer, I'm not just a critic, merely pointing out the flaws in everything— I have a PLAN! And mine is very simple; it has only one step:

FREE SPEECH IS A *RIGHT*— NOT AN *OBLIGATION.* PLEASE, SHUT-THE-FUCK-UP ONCE IN A WHILE.[7]

Sure, we each possess that treasured, unalienable right to free speech, but what about your neighbor's right to live his life for five minutes without criticism? True, it's not in the Bill of Rights, but what if we allowed it anyway— for the public good? We don't need to protect free speech every minute of every day. Any one of us can choose to shut his trap occasionally without endangering the underlying principle.

We Middles know we're hopelessly fucked up by your standards, but can't we have just a few moments of blissful self-delusion once in a while? Until we finish our double-mocha, skim, no-foam Macchiato?

How about this: Each American voluntarily gives up his/her right to free expression, say, 10% of the time. It's like turning off the faucet while brushing your teeth, then turning it back on to rinse— a small gesture that can add up to big savings if enough people do it. This could lower the National Invective Index substantially, yet everyone could continue to rip everyone else a new asshole most of the time. The thing is, hatred and self-righteousness don't dissipate because they're unexpressed, so even if you keep it zipped this time, when the next opportunity arrives, you can still be a fully effective partisan jack-ass at the high-decibel level to which you're accustomed. It's a bargain that can't be beat!

---

7 Buttons and bumper stickers available at— you guessed it— mindyourownvote.com!

But *wait*— there's more! With the time you save by not upbraiding everyone constantly, you can work toward your chosen cause, contribute to society in some positive way, or simply get a life! WOW!

Operators are standing by …

Of course, no political movement would be complete without a song— so I've got one of those, too:

SONG OF THE MIDDLE
(Sung to the tune of "Imagine" by John Lennon)

Imagine there's no pundits
It's easy if you try
No election coverage
No banners meet the eye.

Imagine there's no Carville,
No pfaffing skeleton,
No Coulter and no Limbaugh
No bullshit by the ton

Imagine all these pie-holes
Silenced for all time (woo-hoo-hoo),

  You may say I'm unrealistic
  But I'm not the only one
  I hope someday you will join me,
  And put a cork in Huffington

Imagine there's no Franken
No Hannity or Colmes
No more molten vitriol
Beamed into our homes

Imagine all the people,
Keeping to themselves (woo-hoo-hoo)

You may think I've lost my temper,
But I'm not the only one.
I hope someday you will help me,
Tar and feather ev'ry single one.

CONCLUSION (thank God!)

It's normal to get excited when you discover some Profound Insight. Everyone who ever discovered that same profound insight got just as excited as you have. Before you Change The World, though, please consider trying some of the following options— and believe me, I'm not trying to be a major buzz-kill when I say this. It's just that untold damage has been inflicted on humanity and our planet by people who are every bit as enthusiastic as you. So, please, have a quick look at the list.

CHANGING THE WORLD PRE-FLIGHT CHECKLIST

- Check with The World to see if it's interested.
- Learn something about The World before you change it.
- Find out if your bright idea has already been tried, and if so, why didn't it work?
- Make sure you're not about to undo a lot of work that someone else just finished.
- "Beam" to another world and change that one.
- Get a job.

So there you have it— one man's viewpoint. You can either buy the book or leave it on the shelf. If you choose to read it, you can ignore what's inside, embrace it, or something in between. It's up to you.

In the meantime, I understand how exciting it must be to discover the Perfect Philosophy that will End All Poverty and Suffering, pave the road to Global Peace, or unite all the world's peoples in three-part harmony over a Coke® (If Only Everyone Would Just Listen).

All I'm asking is this:

When you do stumble upon the Key to Universal Truth— keep it to yourself. I really don't want to hear about it. That's because I have my own Universal Truth, and— like you— don't have any interest in, or room for, anyone else's.

The one difference, of course, is that mine is The Right One. And if you don't agree with me, then— well ...

You're an idiot.

A Q&A SESSION WITH THE AUTHOR

Q: Are you some kind of nutjob?

A: Well, obviously. Normal people don't write entire books just to vent about a few pet peeves.

Q: Then how do "normal people" vent their frustrations?

A: Drinking, drugs, spousal abuse and public service, of course.

Q: Most of what you have to say is opinionated drivel, but very occasionally you make a valid point. Have you considered talk radio?

A: Writing opinionated drivel is harder than you think. I doubt I could do this daily.

Q: This is your spouse. You don't seem to have any problem whatsoever producing loads of opinionated drivel. Every day.

A: I stand corrected.

Q: I love your ideas! Have you considered starting a cult following and robbing mindless drones like me of their money, property, intellectual freedom, self-dignity and anything else you can get?

A: You bet. This book is step one, so stay tuned. In the meantime, send me an e-mail with all your personal information "for my records."

Q: This book presents a lot of pseudoscience nonsense as fact— particularly about human cognition. Where did you do your research?

A: I'm not sure I understand the question.

Q: I look around me and all I see is Greed, Avarice, Lust and Degradation. It troubles me a great deal, but despite my prayers to Jesus it never stops. What can I do?

A: I'd suggest you start by trying Lust. Degradation should follow pretty much automatically, and your desire for more and more sex will provide you with plenty of practice that you can apply toward being successfully Greedy (just substitute money for sex— simple). I'm not exactly sure what Avarice is, but I'd bet that it will fall right into place before you know it.

Q: My pastor says you're going to Hell for writing this blasphemous drivel. Doesn't that bother you?

A: Not as long as you and your pastor are going to Heaven.

Q: Why are you so much harder on Liberals than Conservatives?

A: This book is scrupulously even-handed. Fair and Balanced— No Bias, No Bull. If you don't agree, review the section on confirmation bias again, pinko.

Q: Ebony and ivory live together in perfect harmony, side by side on my piano keyboard, oh Lord, why don't we?

A: That's because your keyboard is an inanimate object, not a group of dumb, selfish, biased, hateful people jammed together against their will, Paul.

Q: I travel on a private jet. Can I be involved in environmental causes?

A: No. Why isn't that obvious?

Q: Some people have called me an asshole, just because I drive a Hummer. Does this seem fair?

A: Completely fair, asshole.

Q: When is Alec Baldwin going to make good on his promises to leave the country?

A: Never, evidently. Now he's threatening to run for office. If he gets elected, I'm moving to Uzbekistan. I promise.

Q: Why does Bono, like, wear sunglasses when he's, like, inside, even if he's, like, on some international peace panel, or whatever?

A: So people like you will adore him for being Above It All. Either that or he has photophobia.

Q: I'm young and absolutely convinced that I know everything— yet no one will listen to me. Will this frustration ever end?

A: Yes, when you get older and realize you don't know shit. Then it will be obvious why nobody listens to you. Painfully so, I'm sorry to say.

Q: Who appointed you?

A: I did. I wrote a book about something, and you are reading it. That makes me an "expert."

Q: What if you are totally full of shit?

A: Doesn't matter. I have a book out, and you don't.

Q: So what? Any asshole can publish a book nowadays.

A: Evidently.

About the Author

JC Bourque is a cranky middle-aged curmudgeon who works in the advertising field. His family, friends and coworkers had given him an ultimatum: either write a book or shut up. This is that book.

SELECTED BIBLIOGRAPHY

If you read only two books:
The End of Faith, Sam Harris
The Vision of the Anointed, Thomas Sowell

Books that have a direct bearing on the subject of this book:
The Logic of Failure, Dietrich Dorner
The Death of Common Sense, Phillip K. Howard
Talk to the Hand, Lynn Truss
Give Me a Break, John Stossel
The Road to Serfdom, F. A. Hayek

Books that are generally or peripherally relevant to the subject of this book:
In Praise of Prejudice, Theodore Darymple
Fashionable Nonsense, Alan Sokal, Jean Bricmont
Higher Superstition, Paul R. Gross, Norman Levitt
Crazies to the Left of Me, Wimps to the Right, Bernard Goldberg
The No Asshole Rule, Robert I. Sutton, PhD

Books that I didn't finish reading, but I think I got the basic gist of, and if so, would have something to do with the subject of this book:
Extraordinary Popular Delusions and the Madness of Crowds,
Charles Mackay, LL.D.

Books that, based on their titles and jacket blurbs, purported to be a balanced critique of both left- and right-wing extremism, but upon reading turned out to be thinly-disguised Liberal partisan treatises with only token party self-criticism:
Wingnuts, How the Lunatic Fringe is Hijacking America, John Avlon

Books that I have read in an insincere attempt to show that I performed open-minded basic research about the subject of this book, but which are written by authors who are just plain nuts:
An Inconvenient Book, Glenn Beck

Books that have covered essentially the same subject material and were published before this one, by authors with better credentials, but it's too late because you already bought mine and anyway I would make the case that there are subtle but important differences between those books and mine which would justify my claim that my book is a fresh, new take on the subject:
Wingnuts, How the Lunatic Fringe is Hijacking America, John Avlon
The Great Derangement, Matt Taibbi

Books that I was otherwise enjoying but then ran across a throwaway line about Capitalism that pissed me off and resulted in a mini-rant in this book:

Empire of Illusion, Chris Hedges

Books that have covered similar subject material as this one, but whose author called David Brooks (who wrote a perfectly delightful book, *Bobos in Paradise*) an asshole in the introduction of his book:

The Great Derangement, Matt Taibbi

Books by authors who have been called an asshole in print by Matt Taibbi:

Bobos in Paradise, David Brooks

Books that I have not read, but feel compelled to include because almost everyone I know has read them and swears that they are "Important Books":

The Omnivore's Dilemma, Michael Pollan

Books included solely to convey phony credibility to myself as an author:

The Society of Mind, Marvin Minsky

Books that are just great books:

Bobos in Paradise, David Brooks

Authors that I would read the grocery lists of:

Bill Bryson

P.J. O'Rourke

Roy Blount

John McPhee

Authors who I admire, but who a long time ago beat me out of a job at the Miami Herald that I was utterly unqualified to hold, the plausibility of which was a complete fantasy in my mind, and which I hadn't even actually applied for— but still harbor resentment against anyway:

Dave Barry

Oh, sorry:

ONE MORE THING...

MY "BIG IDEA"

You probably figured I was "too good to be true"— what with all my negative ranting about People Who Profess To Know The Answers. Sooner or later you expected the other shoe was going to drop, and I would expose myself as just another self-important visionary with a Big Idea.

Well, I'm afraid it's true. I have one.

I didn't embark with this as my goal, but once you start figuring out what's wrong with everyone and everything, you're bound to end up thinking about how to fix things. It's only natural.

It wouldn't be fair of me to keep this to myself, especially because my plan, if properly implemented without a bunch of meddling interference from the rest of you, will result in nothing less than the Salvation of the Human Race and Planet Earth. I'm duty-bound to share something that important.

During the course of all this rigorous study, it dawned on me that the various plans fostered by these self-righteous, irritating pedants were missing the mark because they were all starting from wrong first principles. Self-serving ones, at that. These extremists were employing first principles designed primarily to confer legitimacy to their agendas. Let's have a look:

Fundamentalist First Principle:

- Man is created in God's Image and is the Master of the Earth and Other Creatures.

That certainly gives you license to mess around with pretty much anything you want, doesn't it? Well, no wonder!

How about the Progressive Liberal First Principle:

- Man and Society are Perfectible through the Application of Reason and Intellect.

Caramba. That's a blank check, too!

This is where I think they got off track. Now, I'm willing to grant that either of those two first principles is more palatable (and more fun) than the one that I'm about to propose— but I think the preponderance of evidence suggests another viewpoint, and therefore the first principle that I'm running with is:

- Man is a malignant, malevolent, destructive, selfish, killing-machine infestation of Earth, and the supreme threat to everything else that inhabits the planet.

Now, there's a starting point. And, not coincidentally, the starting point for my Big Idea.

If we truly care about the planet, its flora and fauna, and the future of mankind— as we say we do— then we don't need to hold any more Summits, sign any more Protocols, or have any more meetings in Aspen.

We need to call the Orkin® Man.

Consistent with my new commitment to being "Oh, so much more" than merely a self-appointed critic— I have A Plan. This plan, if properly executed,[1] will accomplish, at minimum, the following goals:

- Reduce consumption of resources;
- Reduce greenhouse gases, landfill waste and deforestation;
- Reduce overcrowding;
- Eliminate our dependence on foreign energy;
- Achieve smaller class sizes in our schools;
- Conserve water;
- Lower the number of Starbucks franchises:
- Sequester existing carbon deposits from the ecosystem;
- Much, much more!

---

1 Very interesting choice of words, as you will soon see.

Here's how it works:

Roughly two-thirds of us need to be eliminated, immediately. It's not going to be easy to get this accomplished, and I'm sure that everyone will want the process to be "fair," so I propose the following procedures for sorting out who stays and who gets "redistributed":

Everyone on the planet will begin by organizing themselves into self-identified interest groups. These groups can be organized around any defining characteristic: ethnicity, culture, gender, economic status, height, victimhood, publishing record, taste in music, sexual preference— whatever. It doesn't matter. The important thing is that every characteristic, cultural identity or point-of-view about which anyone gives a shit is represented. That's where the "fairness" comes in: nobody's cultural identity gets left out.

The only caveats are that the minimum group size is three individuals and that everyone must join some group[2] by the Deadline.

For those curious about such things, here's how the math works:

World population:	6,975,993,152
Minimum group size:	3
Potential number of traits preserved:	2,325,331,051

That ought to cover the genome, I figure.

Each group will then decide which features of their race, culture, genre, perversion or whatever are worth preserving,[3] and which one-third of their members best-represent those features.

---

2 Refusing to join a group will not get you out of this. All those who do so will— by default— be joining a group called "People who won't join a group," which will be subject to the same rules, and be tasked with determining which third best represents their recalcitrant genre.

3 Since this is my idea, it seems "reasonable" that I should get to be a member of one of the selection committees. As a demonstration of my open-mindedness, I don't care which one. My committee will, however, be ruthlessly corrupt. Start sucking up now, if you know what's good for you.

The rest will be killed.

Now, here's the "Beauty Part," and the crux of the entire plan. Their millions of bodies— those Huge Bloated Bags Of Evil Carbon Molecules— will be disposed of in the following ways:

- Buried in abandoned salt mines, spent oil pockets and geophysically stable caverns;
- Ejected into space;
- Converted into biofuels;
- Composted for organic farming;
- Boiled and injected underground under high pressure to extract coal-tar, oil sands and oil shale;
- Used as feed to raise a delicious new grade of Prime beef;
- Coated in impermeable resin shells and used to build artificial reefs, flood dikes, and vehicle barriers at government buildings;
- Provided to terrorist groups for suicide-bomber practice.

And these are just the uses I thought of without breaking a sweat. And because *all* of the people remaining at the end of the process will be the cream of the human crop, I have no doubt that we, as a freshly-culled and improved species, will find many more ways of utilizing this abundant new resource. Who knows?— our used corpses might yield a natural refrigerant, or a new kind of Super Glue. No one's ever been able to properly explore the possibilities because of all the troubling moral/ethical dilemmas associated with recycling humans. That will no longer be a problem under my system. It's a brave new world.

I plan to call this new program Global Assisted Suicide (G.A.S.).

CPSIA information can be obtained
at www.ICGtesting.com
Printed in the USA
BVHW041622070819
555319BV00013B/362/P

9 780984 933709